"The result of both substantial research and stylish writing, this is a book that every resident of Long Island should read. I'd heartily recommend it to out-of-towners, too, as Samuel shows that Long Island is not only a microcosm of the American story but also one of its major drivers."
—Harold Holzer, Jonathan F. Fanton Director,
Roosevelt House Public Policy Institute at Hunter College, CUNY

• • • • •

"How did a once sparsely populated region dominated by farming and fishing grow into the powerhouse of the postwar suburban American dream in just a few decades? In Making Long Island, Samuel provides a fresh read of the events that brought success and challenges to what still happens to be 'one of the most interesting and beautiful places on the planet.'"
—Joshua Ruff, Co-Executive Director,
Collections & Programming, Long Island Museum

• • • • •

"Like a cool breeze on a hot summer day in the Hamptons, Making Long Island is a much welcomed, refreshing account of the vibrant and complicated history of Long Island. Not only does the book illuminate the island's development and shifting population over time and space, but it also reminds us that by shining light on the underbelly of the American dream, we are better equipped to reconsider and reimagine it."
Jennifer J. Thompson Burns, PhD, Lecturer, University at Albany, SUNY

MAKING LONG ISLAND

A History of Growth
and the
American Dream

Lawrence R. Samuel

THE
History
PRESS

Published by The History Press
Charleston, SC
www.historypress.com

First published 2023

Manufactured in the United States

ISBN 9781467154970

Library of Congress Control Number: 2023938357

Dedicated to the memory of my parents,
who sought and realized their American dream on Long Island.

CONTENTS

INTRODUCTION

As a native Long Islander, I was especially excited to explore its amazing history by writing this book. I grew up in the Five Towns area of Nassau County on the South Shore in the 1960s and 1970s, making my childhood likely similar to that of millions of baby boomers being raised in the crabgrass frontier of suburban America. While on a clear day I could see the skyline of Manhattan, the eighteen miles that separated me from that smaller island seemed more like eighteen thousand. Visits to the city were magical affairs, and I dreamed of one day living there, never to return to the bland and bourgeois suburbs.

Almost half a century later and my dream of living in Manhattan having come true, I now see things differently. My younger days were in many ways idyllic, filled with friends, family and the craziness of the counterculture era. Trips to Atlantic Beach were always awesome adventures (we typically snuck through a fence and then jumped off the boardwalk so as not to pay the small fee), and the LIRR took us wherever we wanted to go. I rarely go back to Long Island, but when I do, I have fond memories of the area and even think it wouldn't be so bad a place to live. Go figure.

A few million years before our house in Woodmere was built, a glacier swept through that part of Earth and formed what would become Long Island. The melt from the Ice Age left some lakes and a few hills, but it would be the shoreline that made the island truly special. Despite the cold winters, Native Americans found the island a good place to live for centuries, as did European settlers beginning in the seventeenth century. The Shinnecock

A group of reportedly the last Shinnecock Indians on Long Island, 1884. It's clear from their Victorian dress that they've adapted to Anglo customs, at least for this formal photo. *"The last of the Shinnecock Indians L.I. N.Y. / B.M. Franklin, Flushing, N.Y."*

occupied part of the eastern end of what would be called Long Island, although by the twentieth century, their land had been taken over.[1]

In the twentieth century, Long Island became a playground for both the hoi polloi and the wealthy elite of New York City and then a network of suburban towns linked by highways and train tracks. Long Beach and Jones Beach have for more than a century been meccas for both urbanites and locals, and the Hamptons remain a paradise for those who can afford to be there. (The six months I spent in an East Hampton cottage were unforgettable). Some New Yorkers, in fact, think of Long Island only in terms of sun, sand and surf (and that the island exists only between Memorial Day and Labor Day), but there is, of course, much more to it.

More than anything else, perhaps, Long Island (Nassau and Suffolk Counties of New York State) is most notable for its innovation in transportation. The Long Island (or Vanderbilt) Motor Parkway that ran east–west for forty-three miles in the center of the island was the world's first limited-access concrete highway. The Northern State Parkway made that highway obsolete in the 1930s, and twenty years later, the Meadowbrook Parkway added a much-needed north–south route for the millions of new suburbanites (especially those in William Levitt's Levittown).[2]

The Long Island Railroad (LIRR), which carries passengers across the island and to and from New York City, goes all the way back to 1834. It is

Top: An 1887 painting of the Shinnecock Bay by Alfred Thompson Bricher. Given the beauty of the setting and the likelihood that many fish reside within, it can be understood why the Long Island tribe called it home for centuries. *"Sunset, Shinnecock Bay / ATB monogram; by A. T. Bricher." New York Shinnecock Bay, 1887. Boston: L. Prang & Co.*

Bottom: An early twentieth century hand-tinted postcard of the Long Beach Hotel. The "1100-foot-long" hotel with "700 rooms" was quite the grand resort in its day. *The Miriam and Ira D. Wallach Division of Art, Prints and Photographs: Photography Collection, the New York Public Library. "Long Beach Hotel (Long Island), Long Beach, N.Y." New York Public Library Digital Collections.*

A 1924 cartoon of a Long Island beach scene. While the precise nature of the dialogue is difficult to comprehend, the exchange clearly involves romance, something that occurred with considerable frequency at the beach. *Conacher, John C., artist; copyright claimant and publisher, Life Publishing Company. "Did yah quor'le wit 'im?: Aw! coatin' po'try 'bout th' silly ol' ocean!: is that any," ca. 1924.*

the oldest continually operating railroad system in the United States and, it needs to be mentioned, the cause of many delays, cancellations and crashes over the decades. (Although it didn't end in a fatality, the very first train-car collision in the United States took place in 1901 in Westbury.) Since then, thousands of such wrecks have occurred—and an equal number of unfortunate train-pedestrian meetups. After hitting rock bottom around 1970, however, the LIRR's service improved considerably, and I happily ride it whenever I can.[3]

As Long Island is the "Cradle of Aviation," however, its history of air travel is perhaps most interesting. The mostly flat and treeless land of the island was ideal for airfields, and the fact that the population was sparse in the first decades of the twentieth century was another plus. Large parcels of land at low cost were available, making it almost inevitable that flyboys and flygirls would set up shop on Long Island. Mitchel Field near Garden City opened in 1917 and was expanded in 1929, having a very good run until shutting down in 1961.[4]

Although there is literally nothing left of the original Roosevelt Field to see, it too held a prominent place in the history of aviation. Roosevelt Field served an important role during World War I, and Charles Lindbergh famously took off for Paris from the field in Mineola in 1927. The field stopped operating in 1951, however, and Roosevelt Field Mall was built on the site a few years later. Roosevelt Raceway, which was first used for auto racing and later harness racing, also made use of some of the land of Roosevelt Field until it closed in 1988. The building of aircraft, too, is a proud part of Long Island's history, with Republic Aviation and Grumman each responsible for some of the nation's best World War II fighter planes.[5]

Alongside transportation, Long Island's reputation as a retreat for the rich and famous is well deserved. On the Gold Coast of the North Shore, members of upper-class society could be found in and on great estates,

A 1938 poster promoting tourism to Sea Cliff, Long Island, to the millions of attendees of the 1939–40 New York World's Fair. *"While visiting the Fair, commute by land or water to beautiful Sea Cliff, L.I. 250 feet above sea level: No mosquitos: Golf and bathing." New York: WPA Federal Art Project, Dis. 4, or 1939.*

Above: A train wreck in Bay Shore in 1909. A wide variety of mishaps has always been a feature of the Long Island Railroad experience. Anderson, M.J., photographer. *"Railroad wreck on Long Island Railroad, Fifth Avenue, Bay Shore, L.I."*

Left: These trade cards issued by the Long Island Railroad in the late nineteenth century depict portraits of girls along with scenes of New York City, Shinnecock and Fire Island (summer) and Montauk and Great South Bay (winter). *The Miriam and Ira D. Wallach Division of Art, Prints and Photographs: Print Collection, the New York Public Library.* "Trade cards depicting portraits of girls and Long Island Rail Road schedules depicting New York City, Shinnecock and Fire Island in the summer, Montauk and Great South Bay in the winter." *New York Public Library Digital Collections.*

A crowd at Mitchel Field watching airplane races in 1920. Such races were all the rage among more daring and wealthier college students after World War I. *Bain News Service, publisher. "College Plane Races," 1920.*

Yale copilots at the Mitchel Field races. *Bain News Service, publisher. "J.T. Tripp i.e. Trippe & G.W. Horne," 1920.*

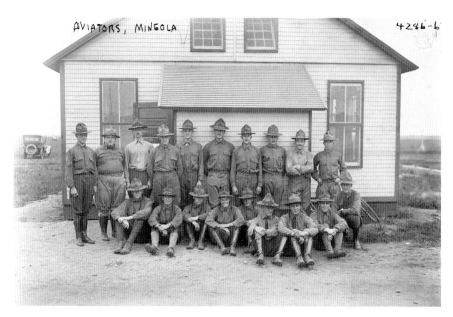

A World War I–era group of aviators at Roosevelt Field. *Bain News Service, publisher. "Aviators, Mineola." Between 1917 and 1918.*

Three military personnel at Roosevelt Field around the time of World War I near the wing of a rather dubious-looking aircraft, at least by today's standards. *Bain News Service, publisher. "Col. A. Miller, Lt. E.C. Kiel, Sgt. F.K. McKee," ca. 1915.*

The British Airship R34 landing at Roosevelt Field in 1919. The hydrogen gas dirigible had just completed a transatlantic flight from Scotland to Long Island. *Bain News Service, publisher. "R-34," 1919.*

summer houses, golf courses, horse and auto racing tracks, polo fields and hunting grounds, mixing with the likes of the Vanderbilts, Whitneys, Guggenheims, Woolworths and Rockefellers. The Meadowbrook Hunt Club was the place to be for such swells, with more daring plutocrats playing polo, racing cars in the Vanderbilt Cup or flying biplanes as part of the Long Island Aviation Club. Of course, F. Scott Fitzgerald's *The Great Gatsby* artfully captures the over-the-top wealth culture that existed on Long Island's Gold Coast before the 1929 market crash.[6]

Making Long Island: A History of Growth and the American Dream is a history of Nassau and Suffolk Counties between 1920 and 1980, filling a major niche in not just the history of the island but also that of New York State and the United States. During that sixty-year span in the twentieth century, the American dream emerged, flourished and then declined on Long Island and across the United States, which is one major story of this book. My goal here is to contribute to the already abundant literature dedicated to what I believe to be one of the most interesting and beautiful places on the planet, countering its popular image as a bland and soulless network of suburban

Above: Charles Lindbergh's *Spirit of St. Louis* a few weeks following the historic 1927 flight that began at Roosevelt Field. Lindbergh Spirit of St. Louis, 1927.

Left: The site of Roosevelt Field in 1957, now occupied by a Macy's department store and parking lot. *Gottscho-Schleisner, Inc., photographer.* *"Long Island Lighting Co. Macy's, Roosevelt Field."*

sprawl where people talk funny. (Pronouncing Long Island "Lawn Giland" is a long-running joke among nonresidents.) Readers will learn there is much more to Long Island than Hampton shares, traffic jams and Joey Buttafuoco. Those interested in suburban and urban history, especially that related to New York City, should find the book to be of great value.

Told chronologically and divided into six decades, *Making Long Island* sheds new light on the development of Long Island and its intimate relationship with New York City. Many New Yorkers went east through much of the twentieth century in pursuit of what James Truslow Adams

A fountain and the grandstand of Roosevelt Raceway in 1958. The venue being used for harness racing also took up part of the site of the airfield. *Gottscho-Schleisner, Inc., photographer. "Roosevelt Raceway, Westbury, Long Island. Fountains II."*

called the American dream. While the term has meant many things—financial stability, making enough money to be able to retire (still often $1 million, despite inflation), working for oneself, having (at least) fifteen minutes of fame, the "pursuit of happiness" or, once in a while, the Statue of Liberty—I use it here to describe owning a home in the suburbs filled with all the consumer trappings.[7] The narrative begins in the Roaring Twenties, when big Wall Street money looked eastward to generate even more wealth from a land boom rivaling that taking place in Florida. While the physical island had, of course, existed for millennia, the Long Island we know today began to be "made" as real estate entrepreneurs recognized the opportunity to be had. Government officials at the local, state and federal levels also invested in Long Island, building roads, bridges and parks to entice people to move there or just visit. Supply for housing matched demand, creating an increasingly linked string of communities that continued to push farther east. The story continues through the shaky

Left: A fox hunt at the Meadowbrook Club, circa 1905. Americans may have rejected the rule of European-style aristocracy, but the elite of the day remained attracted to some of their more sporting customs. *Underwood & Underwood, publishers. "Fox hounds of the Meadowbrook Club—first meet of the season—Long Island, New York."*

Below: Horseracing fans at the Meadowbrook Club House circa 1910. *Bain News Service, publisher. "Meadow Brooke i.e., Meadowbrook Club House," ca. 1910.*

Great Depression and the active World War II years, leading up to the emergence of the quintessential postwar American suburb, Levittown.

Levittown and its spinoff suburban communities served as the primary symbol of the American dream, I argue, as it was affordable homeownership for the (White) middle class that most compellingly expressed the nation's core mythology, steeped in success, financial security, upward mobility and consumerism.[8] Beginning in the 1960s, however, the dream began to dissolve, as the postwar economic engine ran out of steam and Long Island became as much urban as suburban. *Making Long Island* shows how the island evolved over the decades and largely detached itself from New York City

Mrs. W.R. Vanderbilt Jr. (*right, in black hat*) and other well-dressed folks at the 1914 International Polo Cup Competition at Meadowbrook. *Bain News Service, publisher. "At Polo game—Angelica Brown, Mrs. W.R. Vanderbilt, Jr.," June 1914.*

A polo match between American and English teams at the Piping Rock Club in Locust Valley in 1913. *Bain News Service, publisher. "Polo match between American and English teams."*

The exciting finish of the 1905 Vanderbilt Cup motor race in Hicksville. The race was sponsored by W.K. Vanderbilt Jr., an enthusiast of the nascent sport. *Spooner, F. Ed, photographer. "Tracey finishing in the Vanderbilt cup race, for racing cars sponsored by W.K. Vanderbilt, Jr."*

The scoreboard of the 1905 Vanderbilt Cup race. Frenchman Victor Hemery, a European Grand Prix champion, was the winner of that year's race. *Spooner, F. Ed, photographer. "Scoreboard at the Vanderbilt cup race, for racing cars sponsored by W.K. Vanderbilt, Jr."*

A page from a 1909 trade catalog featuring the "Locomobile" that had won the Vanderbilt Cup Race with its powerful 90 horsepower engine. *General Research Division, the New York Public Library. "The 90 h.p. Locomobile; Driven by George Robertson, winning the Vanderbilt Cup Race." New York Public Library Digital Collections.*

to become a self-sustaining entity, making it a much different place than it had once been. Beyond serving as a stand-alone history of Long Island, the work examines the role of the island in the development of the New York City metropolitan area through a regional lens to contribute to the fields of both urban and suburban history.[9] Robert Moses, not surprisingly, features prominently in the story.[10]

While covering much ground, this book focuses on a handful of key themes or areas of inquiry. These are: real estate and land development, specifically home building and the emergence of a predominantly suburban landscape drawing heavily from an urban (New York City) population; the transportation and infrastructural network, particularly as related to commuters and tourism; the island's natural ecosystem and threats from residential, recreational and industrial development; social aspects (i.e., issues of race, class, gender, nationality and criminal activity); economic growth and decline; and wealth culture on the East End. Discrimination against people of color was the norm in real estate circles throughout these years, making social and economic inequity a big part of the story. Long Island's shameful history of racism has been well documented but becomes even clearer in these pages, which reveal a concerted effort made to deny African Americans their American dream.[11]

Sources for *Making Long Island* are primarily period articles published in newspapers, especially the *New York Herald Tribune*, the *New York Times*, *Newsday* and African American newspapers such as the *New York Amsterdam News*. I'm a firm believer that journalists write the first draft of history, and those covering the Long Island beat over the decades have provided an invaluable paper trail that forms the spine of the story. Relevant articles from magazines, journals and books relating to Long Island and New York City help to provide context and locate this one within the literature dedicated to the subject.

Welcome to Long Island.

Chapter 1

THE GARDEN SPOT OF THE WORLD

Undersized Manhattan Island is needed for other purposes than housing the masses of the New York City of tomorrow, which will be Long Island.
—*D.E. McAvoy, 1927*

In 1923, P.H. Woodward, general passenger agent of the Long Island Rail Road (LIRR), waxed eloquently about Long Island in a piece for the *New-York Tribune*. "The future of Long Island is beyond the comprehension of any of us," his guest article began. Woodward thought it obvious that there would be a tremendous growth in population, as the island appeared to be "the natural outlet for the thousands who must leave the crowded city annually." Montauk Point was a natural spot for industrial development, he believed, and the three hundred thousand or so acres of "practically uninhabited land" in Nassau and Suffolk Counties were just waiting to be turned into prosperous towns and villages. "Nowhere can be found such wonderful places for homes, for vacations, for sports of all kinds, for health and rest, for food supplies, and for industries," he told the many urban readers of the newspaper, concluding that "Long Island is the garden spot of the world."[12]

As Woodward was an employee of the LIRR, it wasn't surprising that his article (titled "Observations of Long Island Seer") was more advertorial than editorial. But the 1920s really were a golden age for Long Island, most famously symbolized by the grand estates of the Gold Coast and immortalized in *The Great Gatsby*. While modern times had no doubt arrived—planes, trains and automobiles seemed to be everywhere—Long Island remained heavily rural, more a string of small towns than the vast suburban development it would become. The pressures of the modern age could be felt on the island, however, with a faster way of life and a greater emphasis on money, much of it driven by the city residing just to the west. Women, too, were different than they had been before the Great War, more independent and less likely to be content as second-class citizens. Many men had returned from the war to end all wars in a fragile state, and Prohibition made it somewhat more challenging to find a beverage that might soothe one's nerves.

It was the continually expanding national economy, however, that had the greatest impact on the dramatic development of Long Island after World War I. Through the 1920s, Wall Street gradually picked up steam to the point where anyone with a tidy sum to invest could multiply their money. Large investors formed syndicates with real estate developers, seeing the wide-open fields and declining estates on Long Island as prime property to transform into housing for the burgeoning middle class. Young, married New York City businessmen were the primary target, as these rent-paying apartment dwellers would be most attracted to the idea of owning a home in the cleaner, more bucolic suburbs for themselves and their families. The land boom of the 1920s was steadier than the real estate rollercoaster of Florida in the roaring twenties and laid the foundation for the Long Island we know today.

Quite the Natural Thing

That aviation would play a significant role in Long Island's history could already be detected in the 1920s. Model-Ts were rolling off Henry Ford's assembly lines in great numbers as the decade began, but some of the upper crust were already giving up their motorcars for faster transportation. "Ultra-smart Long Island is right now in the process of bidding farewell to automobiles as pleasure vehicles and is ushering in the privately owned airplane as the proper medium for use in attending afternoon tea and the theater," Quinn L. Martin announced in the *New York Tribune* in 1920. Airplanes of various makes and models could be seen in the backyards of some wealthy homeowners in Garden City, Long Beach, Greenport, and Port Washington and, increasingly, the skies all over the island. Flying enthusiasts, like Lawrence B. Sperry of Garden City and Albert R. Fish of East Marion, were convinced that airplanes would in the near future eclipse cars as Americans' vehicle of preference. "We will go to church in them, to the opera, to our work, to the beach, and to the South in the winter," Sperry stated, thinking aviation to be "quite the natural thing."[13]

Until such a time, however, automobiles remained a relatively speedy way to move about Long Island. Roads in the early 1920s were notoriously bad, however, making any journey of significant length an adventure. Merrick Road east from Queens to Amityville was a common route for motorists, as it was roughly paved, but dirt roads likely awaited those wishing to then go north to Farmingdale or south to Babylon. Already there were speed laws in place, however, with Nassau County's finest on motorcycles ready to give tickets out to those exceeding the limit of ten or twenty miles per hour.[14]

Despite less-than-ideal driving conditions, urbanites were encouraged to see the bucolic wonders of Long Island via an automobile. In fact, one could take a two-hundred-mile round trip from and back to Manhattan, although plenty of twists and turns (and the occasional detour) awaited those who accepted the challenge. After crossing the Queensboro (or Fifty-Ninth Street) Bridge and winding one's way through Queens, one would pass "magnificent estates, parks, country clubs, woods, fields, and seashore," an Automobile Club of America tour promised, an experience that would "prove generally invigorating and refreshing."[15] For those who had the time (and gasoline), the eastern end of Long Island offered city dwellers a glimpse at what was still "wild country." "The landscape is often harsh and grim, with the uplands clothed by a thin, wiry grass, with here and there a clump of stunted trees," a reporter told readers, "a picture worth going far to see."[16]

While the summer was considered the best time for New Yorkers to escape their (pre-air-conditioned) apartments for some fresh air and spectacular views, it was the fall to which Long Island society most looked forward. Summers might very well be spent in the even cooler New England or perhaps taking the Grand Tour, but autumn was the season to see and be seen among the Long Island A-list. Those among that elite were especially anticipating the fall season of 1920, as due to the war, it had been a number of years since it was considered appropriate to exhibit such merriment. The Piping Rock Club in Matinecock (now part of Locust Valley) had arguably the most beautiful grounds of any country club in the country, one reason why its autumn horse show was an event not to be missed by anyone lucky enough to be invited. Golf or, even better, polo at the Meadow Brook Club in Jericho was another staple of the season that unofficially began with the opening of Belmont Park in Elmont. "Soon all the big estates on the island will be opened, and there will be much entertaining in the way of weekend house parties, dinners, and dances," the *New-York Tribune* noted in early September that year, with the social scene shifting to Manhattan in the middle of November.[17]

Although the big estates and sprawling country clubs occupied by millionaires took up considerable land, their collective acreage was a small fraction of the entire island. In 1921, Nassau County consisted of 252 square miles or about 160,000 acres, while Suffolk County consisted of 313 square miles or about 640,000 acres. More than half of the acreage in each county was either devoted to working farms or wholly undeveloped land, however, the remainder being villages and towns, private estates, golf and country clubs and cemeteries and parks. Very soon, both real estate developers and some of the more than five million residents of New York City would start thinking that these unoccupied hundreds of thousands of acres might make a good area for non-millionaires to settle down. Taking an automotive drive around the island, as many New Yorkers were doing, made it clear that this land of seemingly endless potato farms and beaches could very well be a nice place not just to visit but to live.[18]

There were other reasons why it was becoming clear that Long Island was prime for development. While it was not the most reliable form of

A horse show in East Hampton in 1933. The Great Depression was in full swing, but for the wealthy elite, the show must go on. *Genthe, Arnold, photographer. "Horse show, East Hampton, Long Island."*

A 1913 horse race at the exclusive Piping Rock Club in Locust Valley. *Bain News Service, publisher. "Piping Rock Races," 1913. June 7 date created or published later by Bain.*

Belmont Park in 1913. The horse racing track on the border of Queen and Nassau Counties was and remains a popular attraction. *Bain News Service, publisher. "Belmont Park," 1913.*

A crowded grandstand in Belmont Park. *Bain News Service, publisher. "Racing at Belmont Park," 1913.*

transportation, the LIRR was gradually expanding its routes, an attractive thing for those considering commuting to and from their jobs in New York City. As well, Long Island was viewed in positive terms—a reflection of it having been the playground for the rich and famous for decades. This could not be said to be true of New Jersey, which had already become somewhat of a running joke among more sophisticated New Yorkers. "Long Island has always been peculiarly close to New York City in popular imagination," an editor for the *New-York Tribune* observed, thinking "the jests which have represented New Jersey as an alien strand never touched the land of Hempstead, Ronkonkoma, Sag Harbor, and Montauk Point."[19]

The year 1921 turned out to be a record one for home building on Long Island, as a postwar housing shortage in New York City further incentivized urbanites to look elsewhere to live. The opportunity to own one's home rather than pay rent was yet more motivation to go beyond the city limits, even if it did mean commuting to work or moving away from friends and family. Construction firms were doing quite the business in Nassau and Suffolk, building not just homes but also stores, factories, theaters, garages and churches. In Nassau, the most buildings being put up were in Freeport, Lynbrook and Long Beach, while in Suffolk it was Huntington, Bay Shore and Patchogue. The LIRR was carrying eastward not only passengers but also hundreds of thousands of tons of materials needed for construction, such as lumber, cement, bricks and plaster. "These figures indicate how fast Long Island is growing," said the general freight agent for the railroad, asserting that his trains were better than trucks for transporting heavy materials given the state of some of the roads on the island.[20]

The year 1922 was turning out to be even stronger in building activity on Long Island, and by the fall, it was expected to break the previous record that had been set in 1912. While not a boom, there was "a steady market with a constantly growing demand," as the *New York Times* reported. Buyers of both homes and commercial real estate were expected to improve their property, the goal being to raise the value of the larger community. The typical path of suburban development was the formation of a town followed by municipal improvements and then land sales combined with the erection of houses and other buildings. It was the reselling of properties where the biggest profit-making opportunities resided, however, a process that created liquidity for further investment and development. On the South Shore, the Island Park-Long Beach area was following such a step-by-step formula orchestrated by brokerages, which were in a position to make the most money through constant turnover, while Port Washington was the prime example on the North Shore. Landscape architecture and financing were other integral components of this systematic approach to suburban development that was becoming the model for more Long Island towns, especially those near the water.[21]

While the transformation of large Long Island farms into suburban home lots had begun in the first decade of the twentieth century, the escalating real estate market of the early 1920s was understandably getting much attention among more developers. "Throughout Nassau and Suffolk counties the towns and villages are taking on a city suburban aspect, and almost to Montauk Point the region is being taken over as the outlying limits of the great city," the *Times* noted.[22] W.R. Gibson, who had found considerable success developing three thousand homes in Queens, was now looking east as opportunity knocked. Gibson and his associates had just purchased five hundred acres to build "small attractive homes in the nearby Long Island suburbs for the salaried man who wants to get out of the city," as the *New-York Tribune* reported. Two hundred houses would immediately be put up in Valley Stream, Lynbrook, Hewlett and Woodmere (my hometown), with the average price between $5,000 and $8,000. "Some of the houses will be more expensive but it is the middle-class home seeker that the company has in mind," the newspaper added, with Gibson guaranteeing that every homeowner would have a lawn between his house and the street.[23]

HIT THE SUNRISE TRAIL

Not just real estate developers and brokers saw a gold mine in Long Island but also hotel and restaurant operators. The continuing popularity of automobiles was a windfall to those in the hospitality trade who fully recognized the business to be had from motorists looking for a place to eat or stay overnight. In 1922, the Hotel Men's Association of Long Island met in Long Beach and conceived a "Boost Long Island" promotion campaign to try to attract more guests. Tourism had never been aggressively marketed on Long Island, but that was beginning to change as more of the middle class pursued recreational activities like golf and beachgoing on weekends and vacations. The theme of the campaign was "Hit the Sunrise Trail," one of many references to the geographic trajectory of the sun that would be attached to the island that lay east of New York City. "Long Beach should be another Atlantic City," declared one of the boosters, and the possibilities for hoteliers were limitless, even if alcohol could not be (legally) served.[24]

Some of those hitting the sunrise trail were themselves finding the hospitality business to be limitless despite Prohibition. Riverhead and Sag Harbor had become the favored drop points for rumrunners among New York–based bootleggers, who would then truck the stuff back to the city. (Enforcement agents had cracked down on similar activity in Freeport and Long Beach, making the bootleggers move their business.) Large numbers of armed thugs were arriving in otherwise empty trucks and meeting up with the operators of speedy, booze-laden boats on the shore. (The boats had been used as submarine chasers during World War I.) Many fishermen and oystermen in those towns had reportedly given up their trades, finding boat unloading or reselling inventory to be a much more lucrative occupation. There was so much Scotch whisky arriving in 1923 that a bottle could be had for just four dollars a bottle or forty-five dollars a case, a very good deal given the usually high price for decent booze during Prohibition.[25]

The Long Island liquor-smuggling operation was quite sophisticated; ship captains told agents on the shore when they would arrive via cable or radio, who then notified the New York mobsters, who sent a fleet of three trucks for the pickup. Each truck typically was occupied by three men: a driver, a cash-carrying fixer (to pay the unloaders and local officials) and a gunman (to discourage highwaymen—i.e., bandits intent on stealing the load). In recent months, however, open markets were being held on the ships anchored beyond the three-mile limit in Long Island Sound and Peconic Bay, where customs officials could not make arrests. There were rumors that the Scotch

New York City deputy police commissioner John A. Leach (*right*) watching Treasury agents pour liquor into a sewer following a raid during Prohibition. The booze may very well have arrived via the coast of Long Island. "*New York City Deputy Police Commissioner John A. Leach, right, watching agents pour liquor into sewer following a raid during the height of prohibition.*" *New York, 1921.*

was coming directly from Scotland, but this didn't seem likely given that people could make their own reasonably drinkable concoction at a much lower cost. The Reverend Dr. James A. MacMillan, pastor of the Methodist Church in Sag Harbor, was one individual not pleased to see his town turned into a liquor mart—and rather amazed that local or federal officers on the shore were ignoring the whole entirely public exchange, usually done at night but sometimes in broad daylight.[26]

The reverend was almost certainly one of the seventy-five ministers and laypeople who gathered at a church in Riverhead one night in July 1923 to form what they called the Law Enforcement League. The league was declaring war on the bootleggers who had invaded various communities on the North Shore running from Port Jefferson to Orient Point, feeling the gun-toting toughs from New York had crossed the line by threatening beachgoers to leave, or else. In attendance was Sheriff Anza W. Biggs of Suffolk County, who offered to deputize any members of the league (therefore equipping them with the power to arrest the bootleggers). "He had no applications for the job," the *New York Times* noted.[27]

Not only bootleggers but also law-abiding motorists were happy to hear that community leaders in Brooklyn, Queens, Nassau and Suffolk were urging city officials to create no fewer than four additional roads leading to Long Island. Automobile traffic to and from the city had increased immeasurably as Long Island gained more visitors and residents, a story heard over and over again to this day. The proposed Interborough Parkway, Grand Central Parkway, Conduit Highway (later Sunrise Highway) and Flushing Extension would do wonders to relieve the congestion in Brooklyn and Queens, members of chambers of commerce, civic organizations and automobile clubs told city leaders who decided such things. The Interborough would have to pass through a couple of cemeteries, meaning an amendment to the law was required, but that parkway and the three other roads were needed if the interest in traveling to and from Long Island continued.[28]

Meanwhile, there were the existing roads and the LIRR, the latter used heavily by the pioneer commuters to and from Manhattan. In Rockville Center and Lynbrook, two of the most popular towns for New York City transplants, one member out of every two families was believed to commute daily on the train. It took just thirty-nine minutes to travel the 21.5 miles from Rockville Center to Manhattan, at least according to the published schedule. (Delays were common, and crashes with cars at grade crossings, where tracks intersected with roads, and occasionally with other trains would plague the railroad for decades to come.) Thirty-two trains ran between Rockville Center and Manhattan on weekdays (seven on Saturdays), making it easy to see why the town was attracting thousands of what the *New-York Tribune* called "New York businessmen." The neighboring town, Lynbrook (which had been called Pearsalls until a number of newly arrived Brooklynites renamed it by shuffling the syllables of the borough), offered a weekday service of no fewer than seventy-one trains, making it another top choice among commuters.[29]

It was Hempstead, however, that was considered the hub of Long Island in the early twenties, in large part because of the growing number of business startups and manufacturers locating there. A fair number of Hempstead residents worked at nearby Mitchel Field or Curtiss Field, which were also popular destinations among city folk wishing to see the exciting flying exhibitions regularly given at each. The Meadow Brook Hunt Club was also close to Hempstead, a key site of Long Island society offering polo, golf and mixing with fellow Very Important People. Hempstead Country Club, down the road a bit, was the place for tennis and expert golfers (it was exceedingly difficult to achieve par on the new course), and its weekly dinner dance was the highlight of the town's social scene.[30]

Alongside the much-flaunted beauty and festivity of suburban bedroom communities and country clubs was the decidedly darker side of Long Island. As in many other parts of the country, the Ku Klux Klan had quite a presence on the island in the 1920s and were not afraid to show it. The White supremist group often greatly swayed civic and community activities, suggesting that members were part of local government. (The smaller female auxiliary of the KKK was the Kamelias.) The KKK had a certain way of winning contests at patriotic events honoring war veterans, the prize more often than not being an American flag. In East Rockaway and Lynbrook in 1923, for example, more than two thousand members in their white robes and masks marched down Hempstead Avenue, with five hundred cars also in the parade and block party following the contest. (The march passed the Hebrew Educational Alliance, perhaps not coincidentally; not saluting the flag as it passed in a KKK parade was not advised, even if one was a war vet.) Klansmen could also be seen at events in Lindenhurst, Oceanshore, Huntington and Freeport, most of them sponsored by volunteer firemen. There were real fears that the KKK would go further by becoming a recognized political party instead of just a club for those who hated people of color, Jews and Catholics.[31]

Interestingly, Long Island Klansmen were known to join church leaders in declaring war on rumrunners. Like the preachers, the local KKK occasionally tipped off federal dry agents when they heard of liquor going east in vehicles, perhaps not pleased to see New York City mobsters moving into their territory. In 1924, about thirty Klansman in six automobiles on Merrick Road near Westhampton actually gave chase to a car that was loaded with twenty cases of Scotch. After a three-mile race, the two men in the liquor-laden car were detained and then arrested by the feds. The KKK was quite proud of its involvement in anti-smuggling, thinking such law enforcement efforts helped its not very good public image.[32]

There was little that the odd triumvirate of Klansmen, ministers and federal agents could do about a "floating barroom" that was anchored fifteen miles off the Long Island coast, however. The large vessel, which flew the flag of Great Britain, was fitted out as a cabaret ship, complete

A group of female Ku Klux Klan members (*kneeling, in dark clothes, before the leader*) at a 1924 initiation somewhere on Long Island. Their male counterparts in white stand behind them, while spectators watch the ceremony. *Triangle Studio, photographer.* "*First public appearance of women of the K.K.K. on Long Island.*"

with an old-fashioned American bar, a ballroom for dancing, a jazz band from Alabama and other assorted entertainers. A crude reproduction of the Statue of Liberty adorned the ship's poop deck, according to the reporter who broke the story, adding to the Americanness of the setting. Positioned well beyond the three-mile limit, the big boat was brightly lit, making no effort to hide from customs officials. Private yachts surrounded the floating cabaret, which served drinks costing $1 to $2.50 ($17 to $43 today) after a $5 cover charge ($87 today). The Coast Guard was, frankly, flummoxed about what to do about the huge party boat, hoping that Great Britain would call the vessel back out of respect for this country's ban on alcohol.[33]

MR. AVERAGE CITIZENS

While there were many Long Islanders who could afford to enjoy such extravagance, a legacy of the island's Old Money past, it was newer, much more modest money that was transforming the island into something quite different. It was commonly believed that there was more wealth in the middle and northern sections of Nassau County—within a ten-mile radius of Westbury—than any other part of the country of that size.[34] But that was fast changing: the median income or average net worth of households was dropping precipitously as more members of the middle class relocated to Long Island. Builders were, according to a journalist for the *New York Herald Tribune*,

> *reaching out after a population of Mr. Average Citizens, and a great deal of the development there is for the man or woman of modest means who prefers country life, a good-sized plot of ground and a reasonably priced and attractively designed home to such attractions as proximity to the white lights and a subway train every three minutes to Grand Central Terminal.*[35]

The ascent of Mr. Average Citizens was in part a function of the decline of wealth culture in the United States. The war and the economic recovery that followed made it almost impossible to create new estates like the ones that had been built in the late nineteenth century and beginning of the twentieth century, and simply keeping up such estates was proving difficult indeed, even for the very rich. If nothing else, far fewer Americans wanted to be in service after the war; rather than be butlers or maids, more members of the working class were choosing to be company men and women in the pursuit of their own American dream. As well, the housing shortage in New York City was an impetus to seek literally greener pastures, with nearby Long Island often a top choice given the existing rail service. Many speculators were erecting small, low-cost homes in towns such as Westbury, Garden City and Mineola and finding a ready market for their simple but well-made houses.[36]

With the LIRR carrying ever more passengers and freight, its board of directors knew that significant improvements had to be made to its service. In 1924, the board announced a sweeping overhaul of its system, with no fewer than 138 specific steps to be taken to offer a better experience to passengers and builders. From the major (electrifying the existing steam-powered Montauk line between Jamaica and Babylon) to the minor (adding newspaper pockets in hundreds of coaches), the proposed changes promised to turn the LIRR into a literally smoother-running machine. Reducing the number of passengers having to transfer at Jamaica was key, as that slowed the whole operation down, making many a commuter fret he or she would be late for work or dinner at home. New equipment, new stations and eliminating some grade crossings were also part of the ambitious multimillion-dollar plan.[37]

The Nassau County House in Mineola 1917. The building replaced an earlier one and would itself be replaced by a new one in 1940, which still stands. *Bain News Service, publisher.* *"Court House, Mineola."*

Given the consistent rise in passengers moving through Pennsylvania Station since the railroad started keeping track, the proposed improvements made much sense. In 1911, six million passengers passed through that terminal, while in 1924 the number had more than quintupled to thirty-three million. Similar growth had taken place at the Flatbush Avenue Terminal in Brooklyn, with most of the increase there, too, directly correlated with the gradually rising population of Long Island. A deeper dive into the statistics revealed that the number of monthly tickets, which offered a significant discount over the purchase of daily tickets, had and was continuing to jump. Just as home developers had reported, it was clear that commuting to Manhattan from Long Island was altering the way in which many workers were going to and from their jobs in the city.[38]

Not to be outdone, perhaps, the Long Island State Park Commission soon announced its own comprehensive plan to move people about on the island in a faster and more efficient way. Overhauling the roads and parkways was seen as the only real way to relieve the traffic congestion getting into and out of the city, with Governor Alfred E. Smith taking the lead on the project in 1925. Expanding the highway system in Queens was all well and good, but the routes on Long Island were simply not equipped to handle the number of vehicles spilling onto them. Nassau County had to keep up with the city in terms of road construction, in other words, or else, as the governor put it, "conditions of absolute chaos would develop." The proposed solution was a "belt line" that ran across Long Island from Queens, cutting across all the main arteries and allowing them access to one another. Farther east, a "Cross-Island Boulevard" running from Sea Cliff to Long Beach and a "Cross-Island State Parkway" running from Oyster Bay to Jones Beach would make those areas more accessible. If those new highways weren't enough, a Northern State Parkway coming out of Nassau Boulevard and a Southern State Parkway extending from Central Avenue should solve the traffic problem for good, according to the commission.[39]

With new homes, train stations and roads being built or planned, Edwin A. Osborne posed a good question. "How long can the remaining wildlife of Long Island hold out against the rapid extension of the suburbs?" he asked in the *New York Times* in 1925, with conservationists like himself unsure of the answer. Osborne, a field naturalist with the Permanent Wild Life Protection Fund, believed that at the current rate of housing development, it was a matter of just a few years before the remaining animals in the island's woodlands would disappear. Over the past few hundred years of White settlement, the numbers of many different creatures, including timber wolves, raccoons, skunks, foxes and bears, had decreased significantly—if they had not gone extinct. (The once-plentiful heath hens, turkeys, pigeons and cranes were no more.) Quail and partridge could only be found on private preserves used by gun clubs, and legislation to save these birds from extinction had failed. Even the ubiquitous gray squirrel and rabbit had become hard to find because of hunters, although somehow, the red fox had avoided such a fate. Deer, possum and ducks remained plentiful, but Osborne believed these, too, could vanish if unchecked development continued and hunters had their way.[40]

With relatively cheap land, aggressive builders, a burgeoning transit system and an abundance of natural beauty, however, Long Island seemed destined to attract more people than wildlife. A $5,000 house was in the reach of many salaried employees who had never owned a home before, and the promise of more square footage in which to raise a family was a powerful draw. City life may be exciting, but the fresh air and backyards to be found in the suburbs were enticing, even if it did mean sitting on a train for an hour or two each day. "Developments are springing up in every part of the island," the *New York Herald Tribune* noted in 1925, reporting that "places regarded as inaccessible are now blossoming out as sites for homes." The roads and trains leading to and from Manhattan and Brooklyn were hardly perfect, but the city seemed closer to Long Island than it had a decade or two earlier.[41]

The Long Island land rush of the 1920s was an extension of what was sometimes called the "back to the country" movement, which had begun around the beginning of the twentieth century as a backlash to the intensifying challenges of urban life (i.e., population, immigration and industrialization). One by one, the great estates of Old Long Island, some centuries old, were purchased and divided into hundreds of lots, following the classic model of suburban development. Large farms were also bought up by builders or syndicates, as a sizable offer of quick cash was irresistible to many a farmer pondering another season of potato growing. "There is hardly a place on the island that does not reflect in some respect the march of families eastward from the city," the *Tribune* continued, with not just homes being built but also stores, banks, motion picture theaters, churches and schools. Older buildings (i.e., those put up in the nineteenth century or earlier) suddenly looked dated against this new modern architectural aesthetic. Property values were rising, more reason for renters to consider investing in one of the new colonials going up in Bellmore, Freeport, Great Neck, Roslyn Estates or any of a couple dozen other towns listed on the LIRR timetable.[42]

TELL THE WORLD ABOUT LONG ISLAND

Needless to say, some of the superrich with summer homes on Long Island were not at all happy to see nearby estates broken up into cookie-cutter lots for salary men or, perhaps, a park or playground to be used by their children. Millionaires also made it known they didn't want to see one of the new planned parkways running anywhere close to their fifty-room cottages. (One wealthy resident of Wheatley Hill told Governor Smith that the Northern State Parkway would cut right through where he and his fellow plutocrats held their fox hunts.) Politics were very much in play as Democrats and Republicans fought over who had a say in how Long Island should be developed, with battles taking place among local, county, state and federal officials as well. Robert Moses, then secretary of state and president of the Long Island State Park Commission, was, of course, in the mix, determined to carve up the island as he saw fit.[43] Lawyers for all parties were closely studying referendums passed decades earlier to see who had the right to do what with land, with the fate of the island to be determined by the state legislature in Albany and, in certain cases, by voters.[44]

It was hard not to compare the Long Island real estate boom with the one taking place in Florida. In fact, some developers and financiers were making million-dollar deals on both Florida and Long Island, seeing the two places as offering the best opportunities to be had on the East Coast. Ocean frontage was key to making big money, these entrepreneurs knew, and they were thus choosing properties with views of the Atlantic and plenty of dockage space for boats and yachts. (The 100-mile-long and 20-mile-wide island had about 240 miles of coastline.) George Grundy, a Manhattan land operator, for example, was dabbling in both Florida and Long Island prime real estate, most recently purchasing the Phipps Estates for a cool $20 million. The 3,000-acre tract, which ran from Southampton almost to Quogue and from the Atlantic to Shinnecock Bay, was one of the largest ever bought on the island by a single owner. With 8 miles of ocean frontage and the same amount on the bay, the piece of land was ideal for Grundy's aim to create a high-end development.[45]

Grundy and his competitors were banking on the idea that, while homes for the commuting middle class were popping up like daisies across Long Island, the money class was not going to simply disappear. Just west of the Phipps Estates was Shinnecock Hills, where the du Ponts and others

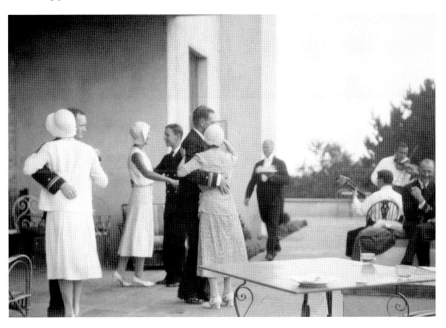

Guests dancing at a party in Southampton in 1931. *Genthe, Arnold, photographer. "Party at 'The Shallows,' property of Lucien Hamilton Tyng, Southampton, Long Island."*

A stars-and-stripes kite being flown by a girl (the photographer's daughter) on the beach in Southampton in 1944. *Frissell, Toni, photographer. "Toni Frissell's daughter Sidney as 'The Wind' in A Child's Garden of Verses, Southhampton, Long Island.*

of that ilk had summer homes; that "colony" had been considered the "Newport of Long Island" since the 1890s. Grundy's purchase raised the price of oceanfront property on eastern Long Island from thirty to one hundred dollars a foot, but investors remained interested in the area. Prices were changing daily as speculators resold property they had just bought, and landowners whose homesteads had been in their family for generations were selling out when told what their scrub brush was now worth. Carl Fisher, the Miami Beach developer, had recently snatched up a big chunk of the eastern tip of Long Island. He planned to build three hotels, three golf courses, three covered tennis courts, miles of bridal paths and a "bathing pavilion" on the land, just the kind of resort where the increasing number of millionaires would like to vacation.[46]

Such playgrounds for the very rich were inevitable given the location and natural features of the East End, but it was the new, modest homes for the middle class that were transforming Long Island. It would be another five years before James Truslow Adams would coin the phrase "American dream," but the concept was already embedded in what would eventually become its central theme—the desire for average earners to own a home. Being happy and having a sense of security were very much part of this longing for a physical, tangible place of one's own, something developers capitalized on when pitching their lots to urban renters. Getting out of the city into the fresh air and sunshine (believed at the time to be a prime source of health for people, especially children) was icing on the cake, and the promise of a clean and wholesome environment to raise a family often sealed the deal.[47]

That Long Island happened to be next-door neighbors with what many believed to be the greatest city in the world made the selling of the American dream that much easier. For developers, choosing Long Island to put one's money into was an easy decision given all the factors in play. Westchester and New Jersey were other good options, of course, as was Miami, but the affordability of land in Long Island, its transportation network and its miles of coastline were just what builders and investors liked to see. (A sandy beach was not far from any part of the island.) The popular image of Long Island as the place where the leisure class spent their summers added to its appeal, and the island's eventful colonial past lent a certain "Americanness" or patriotic spirit to the area. As well, the suburbs were viewed as a safe cocoon from the evils of the city and had yet to earn their reputation among some as a bland, cultureless setting. Sprawl had not yet taken hold, allowing each town to have its own distinctive character and charm.

Builders of the main line of the first railroad on Long Island in 1834 had no way of knowing how their choice of location for the tracks would shape the real estate boom to come. Rather than hugging either the southern or northern shorelines, the line went through the forest area of the middle of the island, an understandable decision in terms of centrality. Among both the working class and upper class, settlement of the island over the next ninety years was concentrated near the Atlantic Ocean or Long Island Sound, however, reflecting the desire to be near the water for either occupational reasons (e.g., fishing) or the recreational activities (e.g., boating) to be had. The center of Long Island was thus more sparsely populated, but that was changing fast as more city folk clustered in towns that had train stations. Developers were focusing their efforts on such commuter towns in both Nassau (e.g., Floral Park, Mineola, Westbury, Hicksville and Farmingdale) and Suffolk (e.g., Deer Park, Pine Lawn, Wyandanch, Central Islip, Ronkonkoma and Riverhead).[48]

By 1926, the roaring twenties having begun as the stock market ticked upward, the Long Island real estate boom had become big news. "Drowsy regions with old Indian names awaken to the cry of the realtor and his high-powered salesmen," Mildred Adams of the *New York Times* told readers. New sidewalks and swimming pools were occupying what had until recently been marshes and meadows, with realtor signs seemingly everywhere. In short, Long Island had been discovered, this almost three centuries after the first White settlers arrived from Europe. Realtors were taking buses of New Yorkers to see available lots, assuring them that a promised land awaited. For those used to hearing loud car horns, seeing the occasional rat and smelling the odor of garbage waiting to be picked up, it wasn't far from the truth. Long Island was an aesthetic paradise, the very reason why the rich and famous had been spending time there for generations. "It is undoubtedly true that Manhattan is out at the elbows and bursting at the seams," Adams wrote, and Long Island was "the legitimate refuge for a crowding population."[49]

The boom (although realtors didn't like the term, as it suggested there would be a bust) was said to have begun in 1921 when the LIRR converted its train to and from Babylon from steam to electricity. The railroad's planned improvements and the pledge for the Long Island Lighting Company to extend its electrical service fueled the surge. In five years, Long Island had become the "Florida of the North," with buyers coming not just from New York City but also the South and Midwest.[50] Still, that wasn't quite enough for Long Island boosters. In 1926, the slogan "Tell the World About Long Island" was copyrighted, with plans to use it in a national advertising campaign promoting the wonders of the island.[51]

What was perhaps most amazing about the fascination with Long Island was how quickly it developed and how geographically concentrated it was. While the island was about one hundred miles long, most of the activity was centered within a thirty-mile radius of City Hall in downtown Manhattan. Bankers, who were financing most of the construction and offering mortgages to homebuyers, made the case that Long Island was contributing to the general welfare of New York City by relieving some of the latter's crowding. The other boroughs could take only some of the spillover from Manhattan, this reasoning went, making it a fortunate thing that there was a big, mostly empty island just eastward for urbanites to occupy. The infrastructure of the city was improving too, as Long Island became a more popular destination, it was believed, with more and better roads being created between the two areas.[52]

The city may indeed have benefited from the rather sudden popularity of Long Island, but it was on the island itself where one could see the vast changes that had taken place in a relatively short period of time. The population of Nassau County had increased 65 percent between 1920 and 1925, and that of Suffolk County grew 30 percent over these same years. The LIRR was trying to improve and extend its service; new highways were being constructed in both counties; the park system was being expanded; new schools were being built in many towns; more local streets were being paved; gas, water and sewer lines were being laid in various places; and dozens of jetties were being constructed to prevent beach erosion.[53] While everyone seemed happy to see such tremendous growth, how long could it last?

A Barometer of Progress

While boosters wanted to tell the whole world about Long Island in hopes more people would visit or put down roots, some strain was in fact beginning to appear by 1927. When a group of LIRR executives went to a board hearing to propose a raise of its commuter rates by 20 percent, for example, they were met by a barrage of criticism. The railroad had previously raised its ticket prices, but its service had worsened, board members told the execs, so much so that some New Yorkers had chosen to move to Westchester, New Jersey and Connecticut rather than face the daily train commute to and from Long Island. "Now you have to fight to live on these trains," said one member, claiming that "it is no longer safe for women and children." Rush hour could indeed be a scrum as passengers scurried for precious seats on the crowded trains. That same board member added that a raise in rates would further retard the potential growth of the island, while another made it known he was not happy that just one Saturday afternoon train had been added to the Medford schedule despite the town's major growth.[54]

Getting to Long Island by car from the city for a day at the beach could also mean an encounter with the teeming masses. While new highways had been built and more were on the way, Merrick Road remained a mess, especially on summer weekends. As well, as soon as a new road or bridge was opened to relieve some congestion, hordes of motorists in pursuit of a shortcut quickly discovered it, adding to the traffic. When the new Atlantic Beach Bridge opened in June 1927 to facilitate the drive from Manhattan or Brooklyn toward Long Beach, for instance, a steady stream of cars (actually measured at four hundred an hour) crawled over it, with little savings in time realized.[55] Work on the Southern State Parkway—as well as the causeway from the parkway that would lead to Jones Beach—was being hurried up, Robert Moses reported.[56]

More roads between the city and Long Island were needed simply because of the fact that there were many more cars in the later 1920s than there were in the early part of the decade. The improved economy had made it possible and desirable for more people, even those living in areas with good mass transportation, to own a car. The number of automobiles registered in New York City and Nassau and Suffolk Counties increased from 357,000 in 1922 to 684,000 in 1926, nearly doubling the traffic. There was talk of a "tri-borough" bridge being built to link Manhattan, the Bronx and Queens, as well as a vehicular tunnel under the East River connecting midtown Manhattan with Queens. (The Holland Tunnel to New Jersey had opened in 1927, and there was speculation about another being dug leading to that state, giving Long Islanders a case of tunnel envy.) Hopes were that such a bridge and tunnel could solve the persistent problem of traveling between New York City and Long Island by car.[57]

It was clear that the population of Long Island had grown significantly since the end of the Great War, but until the 1930 census was taken, it was impossible to say precisely by how much. In addition to automobile registrations, the number of telephones installed was looked to as a way to estimate population growth. Statistics showed that there were exactly 37,508 telephones in Nassau and Suffolk on January 1, 1922, while the number had increased to 87,340 by September 1, 1927, suggesting again that the population may have doubled over a roughly five-year period. Telephone usage was "a barometer of progress," according to the Long Island Chamber of Commerce, which had collected the figures, and a sign that the island was moving into the future with the latest technology.[58]

While the chamber of commerce likely desired more homeowners and businesses to settle on Long Island, it was clear by 1928 that the so-called boom was over. The previous year had been what bankers and real estate people liked to consider an "adjustment period," as the rapid growth of the past five years stabilized. Values were still rising, they were clear to say, but the unprecedented growth of that stretch was unsustainable, which was probably a good thing in the long term. Some syndicates, overeager to buy acreage as a speculative venture, did not find the necessary funding to develop the land into lots. Still, one didn't have to be a Carl Fisher to see that Long Island remained a sound area to invest in property based on its fundamentals, specifically its location between the Atlantic Ocean and Long Island Sound, its proximity to New York City and its network of roads and a railroad. "Continued progress offers assurance that the day is not far distant when the entire length and breadth of Long Island will be, to all intents and purposes, practically a part of the great metropolitan area of the City of New York," stated Edmund J. McGrath of the Suffolk Title and Guarantee Company.[59]

Indeed, the effort to tell the world about Long Island seemed to be working. An investor in Cape Town, South Africa, was interested in buying some Long Island real estate, according to a Massapequa broker, with similar inquiries coming from London, Berlin, Rome and Honolulu. Other requests for information from people in South America, Romania, England and Sweden were being received by a land dealer in Bergen County, New Jersey, making some worry that there could be a "foreign invasion" of the greater New York City area. With the market cooled off somewhat, however, the real estate community was pleased to see potential buyers from "remote corners of the world."[60]

Foreign investors may have heard the rumors that piers for ocean liners were being considered at Ford Pond Bay near Montauk Point. While unsubstantiated, the news reawakened interest in properties throughout the Hamptons, which had slackened a bit. In fact, the LIRR had recently added a special train to run on Saturdays to Montauk and back to the city on the same day. The train enabled those interested in having a summer cottage or staying at a hotel on the East End to inspect a property on the tip of the island and still be able to sleep in their own bed that night, quite a feat in 1928.[61]

More than a rumor was the prospect of creating a national or even international airport on Long Island for both commercial and defense purposes. The island already had a proud aviation history, but the possibilities were endless, some thought. "Long Island is the midway stop between Paris and San Francisco or Chicago and Berlin," F. Trubee Davison, assistant secretary of war for aviation, told a group of Long Island civic leaders already thinking the island needed a bigger airport than Mitchel or Curtiss Fields. It was fortunate that it had taken so long for Long Island to develop, the leaders believed, as now rational community planning could guide where and how to build such a world-class airport.[62]

As the 1920s drew to a close, Long Islanders threw a party for themselves that symbolized the amazing progress achieved over the decade. Sunrise Highway, which had taken years to build at a cost of $4 million, was finally opening, especially good timing given the debut of Jones Beach State Park in a couple of months. An automobile procession along the full twenty-six miles of the route was held, with Brooklyn borough president James Byrne cutting the ribbon in Brooklyn to begin the parade and Lieutenant Governor Herbert Lehman waiting in Amityville with gold shears to dedicate the concrete four-lane highway. "Miss Sunrise" (a beauty contest winner) rode on a float with her maids of honor, followed by thousands of members of some three hundred civic organizations and chambers of commerce along with a bevy of mayors of South Shore communities. Stunt planes flew over the parade, which was the longest ever to be held on Long Island, and residents cheered the procession as it went through their town or village. Boy Scout, fire department and veterans' post bands played as the procession passed, adding to the festivities.[63] Long Island had good reason to celebrate, but a new, very different era in its history was just around the corner.

Chapter 2

THE CALL OF THE SUBURBS

Throngs Invade Long Island Villages in Biggest Housing Hunt in History
 —April 1936 headline in the New York Herald Tribune

I n April 1936, a funeral was held in Southampton for Mary Kellis, who was believed to be 102 years old. While Kellis's age was noteworthy, it was something else that made her death historically significant. Kellis was said to have been the last "full-blooded" member of the Shinnecock tribe, which had called eastern Long Island home for centuries before White settlers arrived. The centenarian had had an interesting life, working as a maid for David Thompson, president of New York Life Insurance and Trust, as a young woman and later for Mary Gardiner Thompson (a descendant of Lion Gardiner, who purchased what would be named Gardiner's Island from the Indians in 1635). Kellis also taught school on the Shinnecock reservation and worked for the family of former president Theodore Roosevelt (whom she recalled as "a weak little fellow"). The woman also remembered the Civil War, the first trolleys in New York City and the 1876 wreck of the *Circassian* off Mecox (during which her brother drowned while trying to save the ship). The Montauk tribe had already dissolved, and with the passing of Kellis, the direct line of Shinnecock was no more.[64]

Of course, much about Long Island had changed over Kellis's lifetime, particularly in the last decade. The effects of the crash of '29 could still be felt across the country, and Long Island was no exception. While for most, the Great Depression served as a rude party crasher of the roaring twenties, many of the island's superrich continued to make excursions to their summer homes or to country clubs to golf, hunt and see and be seen at social functions. Wall Street may have laid a giant egg, but high society still made its elitist presence felt on the eastern end of Long Island.

Not just the affluent but plenty of ordinary folks, too, were going east in the 1930s, however. More and better roads were being built, making the island more accessible than ever. Whether one was relocating or just taking a day trip, Long Island seemed somehow closer to New York City, increasing its appeal. While home construction suffered in the first half of the decade, it picked up rapidly in the second half, so much so that some believed there had never been anything like it before. Automobile traffic also had intensified, with each new road failing to relieve the congestion going out of and back to the city. Many viewed Long Island as an ideal place to find the American dream, but that didn't mean it was going to be easy.

THE GATEWAY TO LONG ISLAND

The year 1929 had been a busy one for the New York State Highway Department, not surprising given the increasing reliance on motorcars as transportation. Long Island received its fair share of the millions of dollars spent, as more and better roads linked New York City with Nassau and Suffolk Counties. Work had been completed on the Jones Beach Causeway, an extension of the Southern State Parkway, North Hempstead Turnpike, Jericho Turnpike and Middle Country Road, and more concrete roads had replaced dirt ones in Suffolk. As well, construction on the Shinnecock Bay bridge at Ponquogue in Southampton had begun, and dangerous railroad grade crossings had been eliminated at Broad Hollow Road, Farmingdale, Syosset, Hampton Bays, St. James, East Moriches and Southold.[65] Manhattanites could reach Nassau County (Little Neck) in twelve miles and the Suffolk County line (Cold Spring Harbor) in another sixteen, a drive that offered considerable sensory pleasures. "Coastal and interior areas offer many charming views, with the delightful odor of pine blending with the perfume of the ocean," readers of the *New York Herald Tribune* learned.[66]

Even ninety-some years ago, however, Long Island locals dreaded the traffic that would arrive every spring and summer when New Yorkers made their day trips in Fords, Chevrolets and Plymouths. And while it was getting easier to go east and west across Long Island, going north and south on the island could still be quite a zig-zaggy experience. As well, speed limits often varied from town to town, making drivers uncertain of whether they were allowed to go twelve, twenty-five or thirty miles per hour. Traffic signals also were inconsistent, and the yellow light had yet to become a ubiquitous feature. Some towns allowed turns on red; some did not. Most concerning, pedestrians had not become totally accustomed to speeding vehicles going this way and that, with many accidents reported, and while some grade crossings had been taken away, driving across tracks could be a perilous experience. Finally, those commuting by car often faced long delays at railroad intersections—this, too, much like today.[67]

Many cars in 1930 would be headed to the new Jones Beach Park (Robert Moses's first major public project). The Long Island State Park Commission was rushing to complete work as Memorial Day weekend approached, knowing that hordes of beachgoers would want to see this heavily publicized attraction. Restaurants, two pools and an immense bathhouse with lockers and dressing rooms for thousands had been built, as had twenty thousand parking spots. A two-hundred-foot water tower complete with colored lights to warn aircraft at night was nearly finished, as were a number of roads and bridges leading lead to and from the Southern State Parkway.[68]

Long Island real estate people were especially happy to see that Jones Beach Park was opening, knowing that it would draw more potential homeowners to the South Shore. Realtors were also finding that local history was helping them sell properties, a sign of the increasing interest in America's past and traditions through the Depression years. Buyers had always looked to the future, counting on the value of their property to increase, but now they wanted to know what had taken place in the past in the area. There was, of course, no shortage of history to be found on Long Island if one looked for it, and realtors visited town archives to pick up tidbits to share with prospects. An interesting event that occurred in the town in colonial days could close a deal, particularly if it involved a rebellious act against the British. One might have a descendant of an early settler as a next-door neighbor, an exciting thing to history buffs.[69]

Stories about the good old days of Long Island also added local color. Some in 1930 were able to remember what land was selling for at the turn of the century; a lot priced at $500 could have been had for $50 three decades earlier. Trips on the LIRR were then bumpy rides with greatly varying speeds, and passengers were likely to inhale more than a few puffs of coal smoke along their journey. There were few commuters to the city (not surprising, since Long Island City was as far as the train went), but

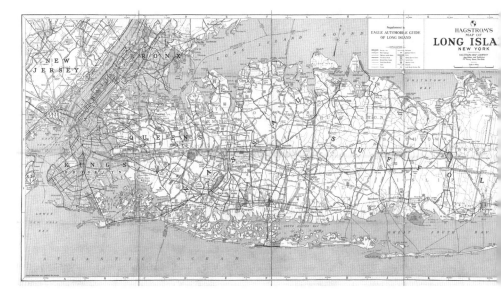

business picked up quite a bit during the summer as tourists made their way to hotels on the beach. Realtors on the South Shore were known to follow the population as it went east, likely starting their business in or around Freeport and then moving on to Merrick, Bellmore, Lindenhurst, Babylon and Brentwood-Islip as more urbanites bought homes.[70]

It was popularly believed that property values were lower in neighborhoods near airports because of the noise from planes or fear of a crash, but the opposite was actually true. Land near Long Island's airports had risen in value, in large part because of its proximity to what were then sometimes referred to as aviation ports. The land on the central and southern parts of the island was remarkably level, making it ideal for takeoffs and landings. (The locations of both Belmont Park in Elmont and Aqueduct Race Track in Jamaica, Queens, were also chosen for their flatness.) As well, airports on Long Island were easily approachable from the sea to the south and west and from the Sound to the north.[71]

Most important, Long Island realtors, like many others, believed that the market crash was just a bump in the road and that prosperity would return imminently. Mortgage money had frozen in early 1930, making real estate activity weak, but some speculators were betting that values would rise. In fact, there were bargains to be had as land became cheaper, especially in Suffolk. Optimists looked to the recently published numbers of the 1930 census, which showed solid population growth in both counties through the twenties. Nassau's numbers had more than doubled, and Suffolk grew by

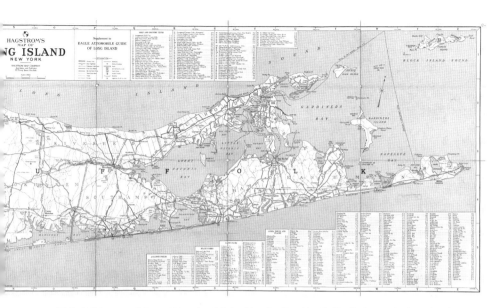

This 1931 map of Long Island published by the *Brooklyn Daily Eagle* was designed to help the growing number of motorists wishing to navigate the island by automobile. *Lionel Pincus and Princess Firyal Map Division, The New York Public Library. "Hagstom's map of Long Island New York." New York Public Library Digital Collections.*

45 percent, according to the census. (Nassau's gain in population between 1920 and 1930 was reportedly greater than between 1700 and 1920.)[72] The economy may have temporarily tanked, but the appeal of Long Island remained much the same, and the American dream of owning a home had by no means disappeared. In fact, James Truslow Adams would coin the phrase the "American dream" in 1931, suggesting that the economic crisis helped trigger a desire to reaffirm what was arguably our core mythology.[73]

The rich, meanwhile, had no intention of a Great Depression interrupting their customs. The horsey set had been coming to Long Island for decades, attracted to some of the most beautiful riding trails in the country. With seashore, woodland and hill country, the North Shore was ideal for equestrians, something that members of the Piping Rock Club and wealthy landowners understood way back in 1912 when they protected trails from the encroaching automobile. In 1930, one could still ride a horse for several hundred miles on picturesque lanes and roads and rarely encounter a car, something members of Piping Rock and other tony clubs such as the Creek, Nassau Country and Meadow Brook cherished.[74]

How long such a thing would last was unsure, however. Despite the economic crisis, work on roads and bridges continued at an aggressive pace, meaning more automobiles would be crossing the paths of horses and their privileged riders. The volume of traffic to Long Island from Manhattan had increased more than 10 percent in 1930 alone, leading highway departments of the state, counties, cities and townships to construct new roads and widen existing ones. The most noteworthy project was the erection of an upper level of the Queensboro Bridge, which was considered the "gateway to Long Island." The bridge was believed to handle more traffic than any other of its size in the country, the reason why New York City's Board of Estimate budgeted $3 million to add a second level. Other projects in progress included expansions or improvements to Queens Boulevard, Sunrise Highway, Merrick Road, Northern Boulevard, Hempstead Turnpike, and Montauk Highway. Making it easier and faster for people from the city to get to and travel across the island meant more tourism dollars for Long Island businesses, a big reason why so much money was being invested in roadwork.[75]

While development of the land progressed, it was really the sea that was driving the growth of the island. The trump card of Long Island, it could be said, was that it was New York State's only open ocean frontage, and it was this that accounted for much of its increasing popularity among both tourists and residents. In addition to great beaches, the numerous bays, harbors and inlets made the place a wonderland for boaters, fishers and others who simply liked to be near salty water. Especially interesting was that by the early thirties, Long Island had become an all-year-round place to visit or live as it became more accessible. For decades, the well-to-do had been coming to the island for part of the summer, but this had largely changed. Now it wasn't unusual for a Manhattanite to take a day trip to an oceanside boardwalk in midwinter to get some sunshine and for the rich to reside in their stately houses twelve months of the year. The draw of the sea made Long Island appealing all four seasons, and even a Depression couldn't thwart that.[76]

HORDES FROM THE CITY

Realtors were known to see the half glass full, and they remained positive on prospects for Long Island even as the number of unemployed grew. In fact, the economic dip was working to the advantage of real estate people on the island in some respects, as more people of lower incomes were leaving the city to find cheaper places to live. While the upper class ventured to

Long Island in the late nineteenth and early twentieth centuries and the burgeoning upper middle class in the 1920s, it was the lower middle class that was heading there in the thirties. As well, some businesses that had been based in Manhattan and Brooklyn were looking east for lower rents, bringing their employees with them.[77]

While it was undoubtedly more difficult than it had been to get a bank loan for a mortgage, the eastward progression away from Manhattan (and the Bronx) continued. Residents of Queens were moving to Nassau and residents of Nassau to Suffolk, all to put more space between themselves and their neighbors and build equity versus pay rent. The exception was the Hamptons, where there wasn't much farther east to go. That decidedly prosperous area was spreading west, making realtors think that development for those of upper incomes would meet that for those of lower incomes somewhere near the middle of the island, an ideal scenario for land and home sellers.[78]

Being squeezed out of this east-meets-west were the large private estates that had, a couple of decades back, virtually defined Long Island. Such estates, especially those between Massapequa and Sayville, were being subdivided and sold as tracts to developers, often at auction. The Lawrence country estate in Bayshore, the Edwin Howley estate in West Islip, the Timothy Nevelle estate in Lindenhurst and the (three-hundred-acre) estate of William Hawkins in Copiague had all been split up for housing, while John Foster's had been converted into a golf course. Some estates, such as that of Elbert Strong, had been in the family for hundreds of years, with the Depression serving as the coup de grace. Litigation was not unusual when liquidation of a private estate was attempted, and court cases could last for decades.[79]

The suburbanization of Long Island made it almost unrecognizable to old-timers who were still around to explain what life was like on the island in decades past. John Dunning, who had worked for the LIRR since 1884, for example, was finally retiring in 1931 after forty-six years of service and told a reporter some of his stories. When he joined the Railway Mail Service at age eighteen, Great Neck was called Thomason, Port Jefferson was called Echo and Sag Harbor was a whaling town (with a greater population than in 1931). Dunning had not forgotten the blizzard of 1888, when it took five days for his train to travel from Greenport to Long Island City. (He and his coworkers actually pushed the train to its destination.) Theodore Roosevelt had ridden on his train but had to go to Syosset because there was no station in Oyster Bay, where he lived, Dunning recalled. While Roosevelt's

A 1955 image of Sagamore Hill, which had been home to President Theodore Roosevelt. *Irma and Paul Milstein Division of United States History, Local History and Genealogy, The New York Public Library. "Sagamore Hill, the home of President Theodore Roosevelt." New York Public Library Digital Collections.*

Sagamore Hill was certainly a beautiful place, most of Long Island at the turn of the century was "pretty desolate then," the trainman remembered, "a sort of wasteland." The South Shore consisted of long stretches of sand with a few fishermen's houses here and there along the beach, a land that had yet to be discovered, even though it was just a couple dozen miles from teeming New York City.[80]

With the official debut of Jones Beach State Park, however, the desolate wasteland of half a century past was no more. In an article for the *Saturday Evening Post* titled "Hordes from the City," Robert Moses beamed about the number of people and automobiles that had come to the park since its initial opening in 1929. More than four million visitors in more than two million cars had crossed over the state-built causeway to the beach, with more than half of these starting out from New York City. While some took local roads (passing hot dog stands, billboards and other "familiar roadside outrages"), wiser drivers chose the much more scenic four-lane Southern State Parkway as their route, where they could go as fast as forty miles per hour.[81]

While Jones Beach was the newest and biggest of the state parks on Long Island, there were ten others that were also proving to be increasingly popular.

Attendance and revenues from the eleven parks were up considerably in 1931 over the previous year, an interesting thing given the hard economic times. More than four million people went to the parks in 1931, generating $700,000 in income (about $14 million today) to New York State. The largest contributor to the state's bottom line was Jones Beach, elevating Robert Moses's already immense political power. With that park, Moses proved he could get massive public projects done and, even better, create an additional source of revenue to fund new projects.[82]

More good news was that Long Island had been, at this point at least, less affected by the Depression than other areas near New York City. Only a few banks on the island had closed in the very bad year of 1931, while thirty-eight had closed in New Jersey and ten in Connecticut. (About twenty thousand banks shut down nationwide that year.) Both building activities and highway construction on Long Island exceeded that in New Jersey and Connecticut in 1931, which could be seen as other signs that the island's economy was not as bad as elsewhere. Finally, unemployment numbers on Long Island were better than in many other areas of the state and country, news that the Long Island Chamber of Commerce was happy to make public.[83]

While most Long Island banks were finding it possible to keep their doors open, the truth was there wasn't much money to lend as mortgages or to finance home construction. As a collection of suburban communities, the island was quite literally built on real estate development, making this a serious issue despite the positive spin from the chamber of commerce. "The situation is alarming, and it is reflected in the steady decline in the number of families living in their own homes," said Michael J. Brady, a developer who was finding it difficult to do his job. Thousands of new houses had been put up on Long Island each year in the 1920s as the population grew, but building had slowed dramatically. People were still moving to the island, but it was getting mighty hard to find a place to live because of the lack of new construction.[84] Older homes were selling briskly, and some families were doubling up in what had been single-family homes because of the housing shortage and as a way to share costs.[85]

While roads were continually being improved and built on Long Island, promising fewer detours and speedier travel, the increasing density of automobiles squashed such dreams. Queens Boulevard was routinely bottlenecked, shortening urbanites' planned days at the beach, and any road in Nassau County during the summer wasn't much better. Sunrise Highway was beat out only by the Boston Post Road in terms of traffic density across the entire United States, a new report showed—a dubious distinction. Euclid Avenue near Cleveland was notoriously busy, but Long Beach Road and Jericho Turnpike were even busier. As well, Route 107 in Salem, Massachusetts, and Route 24 in Kansas City, Missouri, were well known for being parking lots at times, but various Long Island turnpikes, parkways, roads and avenues trumped those, too. In fact, on a Saturday or Sunday during the summer, there were more cars on Long Beach Road and the Southern State Parkway than on Park Avenue in Manhattan during its peak time. A big reason to go to Long Island from the city was to escape the crowds, but it was turning out that the crowds were on Long Island.[86]

Even better news, perhaps, was that the first section of the Grand Central and Northern State Parkways would soon be open for business. In July 1933, a twelve-mile section of the linked highways was dedicated, with a host of VIPs present to cut the ribbon. Robert Moses, Governor Herbert Lehman, Queens borough president George Harvey and other state and county officials attended the ceremony in New Gardens (the eastern end of Kew Gardens), emphasizing that the millions of dollars in land and construction costs were well spent. (Federal Works Project Administration money helped pay for it.) The new parkways (which were also linked to Brooklyn via the Interborough Parkway and Manhattan and the Bronx via the Triborough Bridge) represented, in the governor's hyperbolic words, "the beginning of the end of the isolation of Long Island." This section of the parkways went to Willis Avenue in Nassau County, promising to relieve much congestion. "The day is now in sight when the Borough of Queens will no longer be the bottleneck choking the traffic which leads from the city to eastern Long Island," Lehman added, declaring that more ambitious public works projects were on the way.[87]

The Steady Beat of Hammers

While the city's hoi polloi were no doubt happy to see new, faster ways to reach Long Island, the old guard was likely less pleased. Long Island had been a playground of the Northeast's cultural elite, but it was fast being taken over by day trippers and commuters. Country club culture had not gone extinct with the crash, however, with tennis, golf, swimming, yachting, dancing and many social functions to be enjoyed if one had the cash and connections. "Prominent folk are to be found each morning playing golf over spacious and undulating greens," Robert J. Kennedy of the *New York Herald Tribune* observed in 1933, noting that these same folk "make merry until the wee hours." Members of the already historic Maidstone Club in East Hampton had exchanged their horse-drawn carriages and bicycles for automobiles, but the place remained a prime site for New York society to gather in summer. While the Maidstone Mugwumps (Yale graduates of the club) played baseball against all comers, horse shows were held at the West Hampton Country Club. Golf and other amusements could also be found at the Creek in Locust Valley, Engineer's in Roslyn, Deepdale in Great Neck, the Nassau in Glen Cove, the Southampton Riding and Hunt Club in that town and many other tony clubs. "Gayety on Long Island will continue until long after Labor Day," Kennedy told readers intrigued by the lifestyles of the rich, time apparently standing still on its eastern end.[88]

Most of the Long Island country clubs had been formed by local wealthy estate owners who sought a place to engage in such gaiety with others of their kind. Estates were clustered in what could be considered districts, each with its own identity. In the northeast, there were the Roosevelts in Oyster Bay; farther east around Cold Spring were the likes of Louis Comfort Tiffany and Robert W. de Forest; to the south in Jericho and Westbury was the sporting set, which included Mrs. W.K. Vanderbilt, Payne Whitney and

The Maidstone Club in 1932. Much of the fun continued in the Hamptons even during the worst days of the Great Depression. *Genthe, Arnold, photographer. "Maidstone Club."*

Above: A dog show in East Hampton in 1933. *Genthe, Arnold, photographer. "Dog show, East Hampton, Long Island."*

Opposite: A fashion show in East Hampton in 1933. *Genthe, Arnold, photographer. "Fashion show, East Hampton, Long Island."*

Henry Carnegie Phipps; and to the west in Glen Cove and Locust Valley were the Maxwell and Pratt families and, nearby on East Island, the J.P. Morgan clan. It was residents of this latter area who, in 1912, founded the Piping Rock Club, which specialized in horse shows and racing. Piping Rock was still going strong in the early 1930s; its annual horse show in the fall remained a mainstay among the Long Island elite.[89]

One had to wonder, however, how much longer such days would last. While the Depression had made a dent in country club culture—the freneticism of the roaring twenties was clearly over—it was unlikely that economics alone would put an end to the exclusive pleasures enjoyed by Long Island society. Some plutocrats had no doubt been wiped out, but others had wisely not put all their eggs into the stock market basket or had so big a fortune they could lose half of it and still keep their grand estates and pay their club fees. It was a single individual, however, who perhaps posed an even greater threat to this way of life inspired by the Gilded Age. Since the mid-1920s, Robert Moses, chair of the Long Island State Park Commission (and newly appointed park

commissioner of New York City), envisioned a parkway and park system that encompassed the metropolitan area as well as much of Long Island and Westchester. Two things were needed to turn this into reality—money and land—and Moses had demonstrated his adeptness at acquiring both.[90]

With the Grand Central, Interborough, Southern State, Northern State and in-progress Laurelton Parkways, Moses had laid the foundation for an urban and suburban landscape built around the efficiency, speed and privacy of the automobile. Working across local, city, state and federal bureaucracies was an almost impossible task, but Moses was singularly able to do it. One new piece of his puzzle was the development of four public golf courses smack in the middle of Long Island, part of what would be Bethpage Park. Creating the "Jones Beach for golfers," as it was sometimes referred to, meant turning 1,300 acres near Farmingdale into recreational facilities, with Moses in this case finding federal funds to do it.[91] Moses used and, as many legitimately claimed, abused his power to grab land, even when privately owned. The owners of Long Island estates and members of country clubs understandably feared Moses's proven ability to declare private property in the public domain, knowing that the man's political alliances would carry much weight in a legal battle.[92]

If Moses's vast network of parkways and parks wasn't enough to make blue bloods worry that the good old days were ending, news of an upsurge in housing development perhaps was. Claims that the Depression was over began to be heard in 1934, and it did appear that more money was available for construction and mortgages than during the previous few years. One man voicing optimism that year was William J. Levitt, who with his sons already had an impressive record of successful house building on Long Island. Levitt was delighted to see the passage of the National Housing Act of 1934, which, as part of FDR's New Deal, was designed to kickstart homeownership (and reduce the foreclosure rate). The cost of a new house was going to rise, Levitt warned those thinking about investing in one, so better buy soon before the price got too high. Another real estate boom was coming, he predicted, a forecast that would prove correct, albeit premature.[93]

In the meantime, however, there were great bargains to be had for those fortunate to have a little cash to put down. In the mid-thirties, new house values on Long Island were about half of what they were in the late twenties, making it possible to find a perfectly decent one for less than $5,000. In fact, one would have to go back to the early teens to get a better deal, as land, construction and builder fees were all cheaper than they had been in the last twenty years. Things were quicky changing, however, as major builders like Levitt found it possible to once again develop real estate on a large scale.[94]

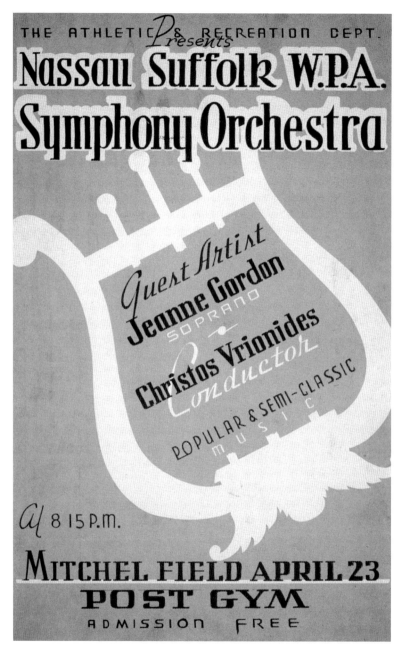

A Federal Art Project poster for the Nassau Suffolk WPA Symphony Orchestra to play a free concert at Mitchel Field. *Gordon, Jeanne, and Sponsor Federal Art Project. "The Athletic & Recreation Dept. presents Nassau Suffolk W.P.A. Symphony Orchestra Guest artist Jeanne Gordon, soprano—Christos Vrionides, conductor: Popular & semi-classic music." Between 1936 and 1941.*

By spring 1935, the economy did indeed seem to be turning around, at least judging by the shortage of summer rentals on Long Island's North Shore. It had been easy for city people to find such a place for the past few years, as many had put off such luxuries. Now, however, summer rentals were hard to find and more costly than they had been. "For the first time in several years, it looks like the law of supply and demand is going to benefit the owner," said Arthur Dunn Jr., a real estate broker, with a recently lowered tax rate in Mamaroneck also encouraging owners to hang onto their houses for the summer rather than rent them out.[95]

Buying one's own house solved the problem and was something more people were doing as new development took off. "The noise of active construction, the steady beat of hammers and song of the carpenter's saw are heard as one approaches pretty towns and villages everywhere on the island," a reporter for the *New York Herald Tribune* observed. "Building and buying are widespread and involve almost every type of house at prices which should meet the financial ability of any man who might be in the market for a house," the journalist added, with the Levitts finding "exceptional demand" for their development at Strathmore-at-Manhasset (which was located on the historic Onderdonk property). The Mott Brothers were doing well in Mineola and Garden City, with what some considered a "boom" in building activity extending as far east as Amityville.[96] Pent-up demand was a big factor in the surge of home buying, as was the much-welcomed ability to have a house of one's own rather than share one with another family, as many had been doing.

While Long Island and the rest of the nation were coming out of the Depression in the mid-1930s, some Long Island old money was deciding to cash in. High-end real estate was changing hands as owners of large, often historic properties finally decided to sell. Mrs. Norman Toerge sold her ninety-acre estate in Brookville, complete with swimming pool, tennis court, stables and brick house, for a whopping $300,000, and J.P. Kane unloaded his property near Piping Rock for a cool $250,000. Mrs. F.N. Doubleday of Oyster Bay also decided to downsize, getting $100,000 for her Georgian brick house on twenty-one acres. There were quite a few other big sales in what Nancy Heckscher of Douglas L. Elliman called "country" real estate, thinking the "frost had gone off" transactions on grand Long Island estates.[97]

The Biggest Housing Hunt in History

One didn't need six figures to own a home on Long Island, however, something fifty thousand people knew well on a Sunday in April 1936. It was unclear why so many decided on that particular day to inspect houses in hopes of finding home sweet home, but the media took note of the huge crowds milling about and looking at builders' plans. M.V. Casey's (or, more likely, his editor's) claim that it was "the biggest housing hunt in history" was difficult to prove but impressive nonetheless. The home hunters hit about fifty towns and villages (including some in Queens) and then pored over the numbers, seeing if and how they could quit being renters. Developers and builders were rushing to complete projects (and planning to raise prices) as demand accelerated in the suburbs. Some golf courses were being flattened, as there was much more money to be made by selling the land than from duffers' fees for a round.[98]

The latest housing boom dovetailed perfectly with the tercentenary of Long Island in June 1936. It had been three hundred years since the first White people settled on the island, reason enough to celebrate the milestone. Governor Lehman led the one-hundred-mile, one-hundred-automobile parade, which started at Borough Hall in Brooklyn and ended seven and a half hours later in Riverhead in Suffolk. Mayor LaGuardia attended the first leg of the journey, with Lehman stopping in Mineola to make one of his three speeches. A century earlier, he stated, it took three days on a stagecoach to travel from Brooklyn to East Hampton, but now that same trip could take just three hours, thanks to the automobile and recently built highways. Robert Moses met the contingent at Bethpage Park for lunch, and then it was on to Riverhead, where more than 2,500 celebrants had gathered at the Suffolk County Historical Society.[99]

The opening of the Triborough Bridge a month later made Long Island that much more accessible from the mainland. (As a member of the Bridge Authority, Moses was involved, not surprisingly.) The $60 million bridge, which connected the Bronx, Manhattan and Queens, led to a new extension of the Grand Central Parkway in the latter borough, which in turn could take motorists to Nassau County. The Automobile Club of New York had long lobbied for such a bridge across the East River to save drivers time (half an hour, it was estimated) getting to and from Long Island. Most of the money to build the bridge (now called the Robert F. Kennedy Bridge) came from a Public Works Administration (PWA) loan that would be paid back through tolls ($0.25 for cars, $0.15 for motorcycles, and $0.10 for bicycles). (It costs $10.17 to cross the bridge today, even though the PWA was abolished in 1941.)[100]

As before, however, the latest transportation project failed to deliver the kind of results for which authorities had hoped. Bronxites were excited about the new bridge, thinking that they now had a quick and easy means of driving to Jones Beach and other pleasant Long Island attractions that summer. That was anything but the case on a particularly hot and muggy Sunday in mid-August, however, when a traffic jam of epic proportions occurred. It appeared that Moses and his colleagues believed that Brooklynites would visit the South Shore beaches and residents of the Bronx, Manhattan, Long Island City, and Astoria those on the North Shore, but that assumption turned out to be wrong. Going east and west was not a problem, but moving north and south was, as Sunrise Highway, Merrick Road, Rockaway Boulevard and Woodhaven Boulevard simply couldn't accommodate all the vehicles travelling in those directions. Getting out of and back into Queens was the problem, in other words, and Moses's new plan to connect the Northern and Southern States Parkways near Westbury wouldn't solve it.[101] That fall, Queens borough president George Harvey announced plans to build additional roadways in that borough to relieve traffic congestion to Long Island, but meanwhile, motorists had to improvise to get to the beach before sundown.[102]

Some kind of solution to going east was much needed given the increasing popularity of visiting Long Island. Hotel operators, local traffic police and gas station attendants all reported that the summer of 1936 had been a busy one, even out in the farthest points of Suffolk. The publicity around Long Island's tercentenary appeared to motivate many to see what the fuss was all about, and the completion of the Triborough Bridge drew visitors from upstate New York and other states. Perhaps hearing about the challenges involved in driving to Long Island through New York City, ferry operators in Connecticut were adding service between New London and Montauk and Orient Point (with or without a car).[103]

Boats were all well and good, but Robert Moses was hardly done building new roads that crisscrossed Long Island. The three-mile Bethpage Parkway connecting the Southern State Parkway at Massapequa with Bethpage State Park in Farmingdale opened in November 1936, with a long line of cars eager to use it on the very first day of service. Not just cars but also more than two thousand people attended the ceremony for the debut of that parkway, with the obligatory tape stretched across the road to be cut by a dignitary. Moses was there, of course, but talked more about building future roads than the brand-new one. Extending the Meadowbrook Parkway was in the works now that the land needed to directly link the Southern and Northern State Parkways had been acquired. Moses's ulterior motive for that road was to provide a direct artery between the upcoming world's fair in Flushing and Jones Beach State Park. Each was a pet project, creating a kind of synchronicity that must have greatly pleased the man.[104]

No doubt also pleasing to Moses was the tribute Long Islanders gave him in April 1937. Moses was referred to as a "dreamer-planner-doer" at the testimonial dinner held at the Hotel Pennsylvania in Manhattan. More than one thousand people attended the event, with speeches made by former governor (and close ally) Alfred E. Smith and ex–New York City police commissioner Grover A. Whalen (who would head up the world's fair). Accordion players, acrobats, a dancing sister team and "voodoo dancers" served as entertainment, but it was the gold medal presented to Moses by the American Scenic and Historic Preservation Society that was the highlight of the dinner, which was orchestrated by the Long Island Association. "Bob," as he was consistently referred to by the speakers, deserved full credit for the development of the island's park system and was recognized as "one of the most distinguished and efficient public servants in the United States of the present generation." Moses had quarreled, to put it gently, with the supervisors of Nassau and Suffolk Counties and estate owners on the North Shore when building his parkways, but all now seemed forgiven.[105]

There seemed to be no end to Robert Moses's good fortune in the 1930s with regard to the development of Long Island. A couple of months after his testimonial, William K. Vanderbilt handed over the rights to the Long Island Motor Parkway to five government agencies, all of which Moses had some control over. The road stretched for more than fifty miles from Flushing to Lake Ronkonkoma, making it a key prize in terms of further vehicularizing the island. Vanderbilt's offer was a generous one, but the backstory was that with its fifty-cent toll, the road could no longer compete with the free state and county parkways that now traversed Nassau and Suffolk Counties. (The term *freeway* had been recently coined.) Vanderbilt made the offer directly to Moses at the office of the Long Island State Park Commission in Babylon, the latter saying he was "inclined" to accept it. While the location of the one-hundred-foot Motor Parkway was excellent, it was in rough shape and needed considerable improvement to withstand heavy use. The parkway was the site of the Vanderbilt Cup automobile race between 1908 and 1910, and after World War II, it was opened to the public as a toll road.[106]

Moses soon accepted the offer, of course, turning his thoughts to how exactly it should be used. Some of it would serve as a connection with existing highways, other parts of it as an extension of such highways and still other parts of it would be abandoned. Whatever the details, the goal was to utilize the gift as another fast-travel east–west route for passenger and commercial traffic rather than reserving it for local use. To do the latter would be to "sabotage an opportunity that will never again knock at the door of Long Islanders," a report by the Regional Plan Commission in charge of the project read.[107]

The news that there would be a major free road through the midsection of the island made residents of New York City more intrigued about moving to the suburbs to the east. "City dwellers are reported interested in country," readers of the *New York Herald Tribune* were told, with "the call of the suburbs heard." Potential home buyers were particularly interested in the North Shore, as that area had already become quite accessible with the opening of the Grand Central–Northern State Parkway and widening of Northern Boulevard. Long Island was popularly believed to be as flat as a pancake, but the North Shore actually had some beautiful wooded hills, a feature that builders and brokers were quick to point out. Harbor Hills in Port Washington rose to 391 feet above sea level, one of the reasons why the Mackay, Brady and Whitney estates had been built in the vicinity. One could even see the Manhattan skyline and, on a clear day, the George Washington Bridge from that point, making selling homes there like catching fish in a barrel.[108]

Potato Fields and Cabbage Patches

The Long Island real estate community was not reluctant to express gratitude to the man who was instrumental in its earning a good living. Moses's creation of state parks helped beautify the island, agents and brokers agreed, and his building of parkways did much to open up some off-the-beaten-track areas for development. Long Island was geographically diverse, but Moses was credited with figuring out how to worm highways around hills and valleys, large towns and small villages and both lakes and rivers. The island was once thought of as having three distinct topographies—sandy dunes, inlets and bays on the South Shore; hills and rugged country on the North Shore; and plateau farming land in the center—but by the late thirties, those divisions had blurred, as highways pieced the regions together. People from the city would not have bought homes on Long Island if it weren't for Robert Moses, most builders and realtors believed; the man's well-documented bullying tactics to get what he wanted were deemed beside the point.[109]

The year 1937 was a record one for the island's state parks, yet more reason to acknowledge Moses's determination and ability to get things done. Attendance was well over six million visitors, half a million more than the previous year. Jones Beach accounted for about two-thirds of total attendance, its sheer size and extraordinary facilities putting it in a league of its own. Wildwood, Hecksher and the other smaller shore parks were certainly charming, but they lacked the wow factor that made a trip to Jones Beach an unforgettable experience. Many wanted to have that experience, even if it meant a hellish drive from somewhere in the city or upstate. There was officially parking space for fifteen thousand cars at Jones Beach, but one day, twenty-three thousand somehow squeezed in, putting beachgoers together in a manner not unlike Coney Island. Those wanting to avoid such crowds could venture to the eastern end of Jones Beach, however, which remained quite wild, even desolate.[110]

With Jones Beach complete and even more successful than anticipated, Moses focused much of his attention on the upcoming world's fair in Flushing. (The site had been the "valley of ashes" in Fitzgerald's *The Great Gatsby*, more specifically the Corona Dump that Moses had wanted to clean up since he was a child.) In Queens, many believed that the fair would have a significant impact on nearby Nassau County in terms of both real estate and transportation. Many of Moses's projects in the last few years had something to do with the fair, as he envisioned the event as a singular opportunity to focus the attention of much of the world on New York City and its environs. John W. McKeown, a builder and developer of properties in Bay Shore, Islip and Brentwood, also saw the fair as much more than a big trade exhibition. The roads, highways, bridges and tunnels that had been constructed in part because of the fair would bring the city and Long Island closer together, he thought, much like how the Williamsburg and Queensboro Bridges and Penn Station linked Manhattan with Brooklyn and Queens in the early twentieth century. The population of Nassau and Suffolk Counties had also grown during these years, with McKeown attributing the gain to those infrastructural developments. The world's fair was going to have a lasting impact on Long Island, he predicted, good news for people like himself who built and sold houses there.[111]

Another Long Island developer, Patrick J. Callan, felt similarly. The site of the fair was close to Long Island's North Shore, making him think that a boom akin to that which took place there in the late 1920s was in the wings. People from far and wide (as well as Manhattanites who rarely left their borough) would come to the fair and realize how close pretty towns like Great Neck, Roslyn and Port Washington were. It was easy for visitors to see that owning a nice house in what had been called the Gold Coast at the turn of the century was within reach, both geographically and financially, Callan believed—a reasonable assumption.[112]

Builders like McKeown and Callan were happy to see that there would be a Long Island regional exhibit at the fair's New York State Building, which would give visitors a good look at the big island that lay east of New York City. A Long Island-at-the-Fair Committee (part of the Long Island Association) composed of business and other leaders was raising $40,000 to showcase the resources and attractions of the island (which included Brooklyn and Queens). Through the exhibit (one of a dozen to be included in the New York State Building), the committee sought to tell the story of Long Island's fascinating past, impressive present and future possibilities. A giant map and oversized mural photographs were planned, as were two animated dioramas—one of Jones Beach and the other depicting various sports activities. A booklet about Long Island was also in the works, with plans to distribute it at the fair and at a to-be-built kiosk at Penn Station in Manhattan.[113]

While trips to the world's fair did indeed stir interest in Long Island, including its real estate, it was more practical matters that created the kind of demand that McKeown and Callan anticipated. Interest rates dropped in early 1939, incentivizing building syndicates to try to acquire land for development. As well, banks were again lending money to borrowers for modest home mortgages, which were insured by the Federal Housing Administration (FHA). These factors led to a revival in real estate activity that recalled the frenzy of the roaring twenties. "Farmers have suddenly discovered potato fields and cabbage patches have a value far in excess of what they have produced for them as gardens," M.V. Casey of the *New York Herald Tribune* noted. Farmers had, not that long ago, been eager to sell out as the FDR administration enacted price controls on food production, but now they were holding onto their land as the bids continued to rise.[114]

Not just farmland but prime North Shore property was part of this latest surge. The Clarence Mackay estate in Roslyn had just been put on the market, attracting speculative builders like bees to honey. Every Sunday (despite the spring rains), potential home buyers, too, were flocking to the North Shore to take a look at existing developments. The low mortgage interest rates offered by savings banks were matched by low rates paid on deposits, yet more reason to invest one's money in property. As well, through its insured mortgage program, the FHA was essentially subsidizing homeownership by guaranteeing lenders they would receive 3 percent government bonds in equivalent value should a borrower default, an offer most banks couldn't refuse.[115] Small down payments and low monthly installments were other ways the FHA was making it easy to buy a house (as long as one was White).

As the Long Island suburbs became ever more accessible due to Robert Moses's roadbuilding to and from Flushing, Nassau County was now running neck and neck in home construction with Queens, which had been one of the hottest real estate markets in the country over the last few years. Since 1936, banks and other financial institutions had loaned home buyers and builders about $84 million in Nassau, according to the FHA, with gain in population of about one hundred thousand in the county over that three-year period. About 7,500 new one-family homes had been built and another 2,000 were under construction, evidence of the nationwide economy recovery of the late 1930s. Renters from the city tended to first look at houses in Brooklyn and Queens because of their proximity to Manhattan and then make the leap to Nassau because of the better values to be had. Central Nassau—Lynbrook, Valley Stream, Malverne, Hempstead, Freeport and Rockville Centre—had drawn most of the new building, but Floral Park, New Hyde Park and Mineola had also attracted considerable numbers of buyers.[116]

While business was very good, it was impossible to ignore the dark clouds appearing on the horizon. Hitler had invaded Poland in September, and a couple of days later, Britain and France declared war on Germany. Another world war, should it become one, would be disastrous for many reasons, one of them being the effect it would have on home construction. Those who had been in the business for a couple of decades or more remembered how the Great War had put on hold the budding development of Long Island and feared that another war would stall the current good times. Indeed, top builders were already rushing to file plans and put up as many houses as possible before materials—especially iron, copper, lead and lumber—became scarce and very costly. Wiring, cement and brick were expected to go up next, as it was known that the military relied heavily on such things for its own building needs. The FDR administration (along with Republican leaders) was saying that the United States would remain neutral, but things were getting progressively worse in Europe.[117] No one could anticipate what lay in store for the United States and the world in the next few years, as Long Islanders joined the fight to preserve the American dream.

Chapter 3

GOD'S COUNTRY

An economic and sociological shift, on a scale and at a tempo such as this country has seldom seen since the closing of its western frontier, is now taking place on Long Island under the very nose of New York City.
—*Frederick Graham, 1949*

On February 1, 1948, a small bit of news appeared in the back of the *New York Herald Tribune*. "Levitt & Sons have purchased 219 acres on Hempstead Turnpike at Wantagh Avenue in Levittown, L.I.," the article read, adding that the parcel of land would permit the construction of one thousand more houses in that development. Little did editors of the newspaper and its readers realize that the purchase would forever alter the physical and cultural landscape of not just Long Island but also the nation and even the world.[118]

With the Second World War, the nation's economy had fully recovered. As in most parts of the country, employment was way up on Long Island in the early 1940s, especially at the defense plants producing aircrafts or parts for them. While for many, the American dream of owning a home was put on hold during the wartime emergency, it was expected that Long Island would have a real estate boom rivaling that of the 1920s as soon as peace was declared. "The desire for a home will continue to grow until peace has come, when there will be a rush on builders," the *New York Herald Tribune* noted in 1942. One man in particular would make that prediction come true.[119]

A NUMBER OF WEEPING WOMEN

Until then, however, there were always more roads for Robert Moses to build. The second season of the 1939–40 New York World's Fair was viewed as additional rationale to add more routes throughout the metropolitan area, some of them leading to Long Island. The Belt Parkway, which connected Shore Road in Brooklyn with Sunrise Highway, opened in July 1940 and the Queens-Midtown Tunnel in November that year. Considerable improvements had been made to a number of roads in Queens, with hopes that the annual summer scrum in the borough would be lessened. Traffic to and from Rockway Beach on any given Sunday during the season was as bad as anywhere in the city.[120]

The rush to build houses on Long Island that had begun in 1939 continued through the following year. A Long Island builder was exhibiting small, inexpensive model homes at the fair, helping to stir interest in the real ones in North Bellmore.[121] The consensus was that construction costs were going to rise soon even if the United States didn't enter the war, as such materials were already needed badly in Europe. Buyers were moving fast as well, fully believing developers' warnings that they had better get that house in the suburbs before it was too late. FHA mortgage money was still available but likely not for much longer, as a world war looked more likely. The Germans certainly didn't realize that when they invaded Belgium and France, they would motivate some people to buy a house on Long Island, but that is what happened.[122]

It isn't known how many fairgoers during the first season moved to or visited Long Island as a result of the fifty thousand booklets distributed by the Long Island Association at the New York State Building, but the regional committee decided it was worth doing again. Like the 1939 edition, the 1940 booklet used text and photos to feature the island's attractions and resources, although the latter included more descriptions of the counties, towns and villages. In addition to what it was best known for—great state parks and excellent fishing—Long Island was proud of its past, with much for vacationers to learn at its various museums, historical societies and libraries.[123] The Automobile Club of New York also recommended historical tours of the island, telling weekend motorists they would find the contrast between "modern communities and relics and reminders of the past" quite interesting. Indeed, amid the suburban setting, a tourist could come upon the location of Captain Kidd's buried treasure, Daniel Webster's summer house and the very home where the lyrics to the song "Home, Sweet, Home" were written.[124]

While fairgoers enjoyed all there was to see at the "World of Tomorrow" in Flushing (now Flushing Meadows–Corona Park), the world of today was continuing to affect life on Long Island. Refugees from Europe were arriving in the United States, some of them in Long Island. In July 1940, eight English children were taken in by Mrs. Daniel Guggenheim, whose Hempstead House estate in Sand Points offered plenty of room to explore. Slides and swings had been made for the children, who ranged in age from one to ten years old. Although they found the summer on Long Island too hot for their liking, the refugees were safe from German bombs, and plans were made to send more children in danger to the estate before individual homes were found for them. Hempstead House was designed to resemble Killarney Castle in Ireland, and its English butler had worked there since the stone mansion first opened its doors in 1905.[125]

By early 1941, Italy had joined forces with Germany, and the United States had aggressively expanded its defense program. About $150 million in government contracts had already been awarded to companies in and around Farmingdale to build airplane engines and pursuit and bombing

The interior of one of Grumman Aircraft's buildings in Bethpage in 1940. The company and its competitors would soon be churning out planes for use by the military. *Gottscho-Schleisner, Inc., photographer. "Grumman Aircraft Engineering Corp., Bethpage, Long Island. Interior II."*

A Federal Art Project poster for Home Defense Day, to be held at Adelphi College in Garden City in May 1941. The event, targeted to women, offered exhibits, demonstrations and instructions designed to prepare a household for possible war. Federal Art Project, sponsor. "*Defense! Long Island women: Home defense day: Exhibits—demonstrations—lectures—drills—music//JD.*"

planes. (The Republic, Brewster, Grumman, Ranger and Liberty factories were all located in the area.) Many thousands of employees would be required to fulfill current contracts, experts believed, an industrial expansion that could alter the mostly residential and recreational landscape of Long Island. Nassau and Suffolk County officials weren't quite sure how to accommodate the presence of giant manufacturing plants amid suburban neighborhoods and golf courses, wondering if they should try to create a designated zone for industries whose workers lived in neighboring towns.[126]

With rentals scarce, FHA-financed housing for defense workers was in full stride. In Nassau County, new single-family homes were going up fast in not just Farmingdale but also Westbury, Hicksville, Bethpage and Massapequa, and some existing properties were being remodeled as well. Similar activity was taking place in Huntington, Copaigue and Babylon in Suffolk, with banks and builders cooperating to keep mortgage payments manageable. More workers were arriving every day, and it was believed that an additional ten thousand would be hired by the end of 1941. Houses were being sold faster than they could be built, but all parties involved were doing everything they could to create communities wherever there was a plot of land that could be filled (and, of course, making a ton of money in the process).[127]

While the bombing of Pearl Harbor in Oahu, Hawaii, in December was thousands of miles away, many Long Islanders feared their island could be next. Days after the attack and the entry of the United States in the war, Long Island residents, particularly those on the eastern end, scanned the skies and listened for the sound of airplane engines. With Mitchel Field and its surrounding airplane manufacturing companies, central Long Island could be a prime target, it was reasonably assumed, almost the aviation equivalent of Pearl Harbor. A (false) radio bulletin that enemy planes had been sighted off the coast of New England and were headed to New York— certainly a prime target—caused genuine panic despite reports from the army and navy that the rumor could not be confirmed. The (true) news that all planes from Mitchel Field were in the air and all civilian personnel were being evacuated from the field was hardly comforting. Soldiers at the field, some with bayonets and others with machine guns, took up positions at all entrances, prepared for a possible attack by parachute.[128]

Meanwhile, in various towns and villages on Long Island, fire sirens and church bells rang out and civilian defense volunteers were called to report by telephone, police squad cars or messengers. Air-raid wardens ordered people outside to go indoors until an all clear was sounded. Schools were closed, children were sent home and there was soon a steady stream of

Air Corps technicians practicing their infantry skills at Mitchel Field around 1942. *Mitchel Field, New York. "Air Corps technicians must be expert in the handling of infantry weapons. Members of an airbase squadron learning to wage hand-to-hand combat with bayonets under the tutelage of Captain Clifford W. Vedder, squadron commander."*

cars leaving the island. In Bay Shore, a journalist on the scene reported, "a number of weeping women," clutching their children, wandered the streets until police and wardens told them to go home. In Amityville, motorists were ordered to move their parked cars off the highway to side streets, and in Babylon, groups of people gathered at the municipal building to get the latest news. Roads near the airplane factories in Farmingdale and Bethpage were blocked off, as were all routes leading to Mitchel Field.[129]

One Mitchel Field pilot scanning the skies was Flying Cadet Joseph Rybak, who was attached to the Thirty-Third Pursuit Group of the Fifty-Eighth Squadron. Just one day after Pearl Harbor, Ryback was piloting a P-40 Curtiss pursuit plane when it experienced engine trouble 1,500 feet over Lindenhurst. Over the radio, he was instructed to make a forced landing in any clear spot. Ryback chose what appeared to be an open space in the north end of Montefiore Cemetery, near the Southern State Parkway Extension. Ryback glided the plane down but clipped the nine-foot hedge that bordered the cemetery. From his vantage point, the pilot was unable to see the eight people and the two cars over the hedge. Two of the group saw the plane approaching and safely ducked under its left wing. Four others were struck by the wing and had various bones broken by it, including the cemetery's superintendent. One man's skull was fractured by the wing, however, and he was soon dead from his injuries. (The wing also cut in two the group's station wagon and overturned the superintendent's vehicle.) The plane proceeded to bounce five hundred yards into the cemetery before stopping, and Ryback was taken to the hospital at Mitchel Field with a possible skull fracture.[130]

On New Year's Day 1942, some other Long Islanders were vividly reminded that the country was at war. Lieutenant Charles Van Eeuwen had taken off early one morning from Mitchel Field in a Douglas bomber on a routine training flight with five airmen on board. Over Mineola, early risers could see that the plane was in trouble. The pilot had a tough choice

Female military personnel at Mitchel Field in 1943. *Aumuller, Al, photographer. "Col. Oveta Culp Hobby right talks with Auxiliary Margaret Peterson and Capt. Elizabeth Gilbert at Mitchel Field/World Telegram & Sun."*

An entrance to the Montifiore Cemetery in Pinelawn in 1958. *Gottscho-Schleisner, Inc., photographer. "New Montifiore Cemetery, Pinelawn, Long Island, New York. Gate II."*

to make in deciding where to make a crash landing. There was some level ground ahead, the twenty-two-year-old from Michigan could see, but it was surrounded by hundreds of houses in the Hillside Heights neighborhood. A couple thousand feet before that was a sandpit surrounded by steep banks, almost ensuring that nobody on the ground would be hurt or killed by a crash. Heroically, Van Eeuwen chose the latter option, which made it far less likely that he and his fellow airmen would survive. The lieutenant steered the bomber into the pit, which was 150 feet below street level, attempting to make a pancake landing. On impact, the plane caught fire and exploded when the gasoline tank ignited. Flaming parts of the bomber flew in all directions for a good distance, and all five crewmen were killed instantly. The sound from the crash woke up many residents, the windows of houses of several nearby towns shook and police headquarters was flooded with phone calls.[131]

Forget It

The war continued to make itself felt on Long Island in the water as well as the air. In January 1942, a rumor circulated that an enemy sub had torpedoed an oil tanker within sight of land off Hampton Bays. Coast Guard boats went through heavy seas, while navy planes flew overhead in search of survivors or signs of wreckage. Residents of Quogue, meanwhile, went down to the beach to repel a potential submarine attack (recalling the plot of the comedic 1979 movie *1941*). It was initially unclear whether there had been an attack, but the situation was understandably tense given the actual torpedoing of the Panamanian oil tanker *Norness* a few days earlier, sixty miles southeast of Montauk Point. Sailors on the German U-boat had machine-gunned a life raft sent from the *Norness*, which was the first ship to be sunk off the Atlantic coast in World War II.[132] The following day, it was confirmed that a second ship had been sunk by a U-boat. Survivors of the British tanker *Coimbra* were being picked up near where the *Norness* had gone down, but the navy wasn't saying much more than that.[133]

U-boats off the coast were not preventing more people, especially defense workers, from moving to Long Island, at least for the war emergency. The thousands of employees making airplanes or their parts were earning good money—many of them for the first time ever or in more than a decade—making a home of one's own within reach. Just as predicted, however, materials for house construction had become difficult to source, limiting the number of new homes that could be built. Labor, too, was getting increasingly hard to find, as more men enlisted or found higher-paying jobs in defense plants. Still, many were saying that this war would be a short one now that America had joined the Allies and that an even bigger and better postwar boom was right around the corner.[134]

Interestingly, some on the mainland had come to believe that Long Island had, because of the war, become one big military camp. People knew that airplanes were built and flown there, which perhaps led to the idea that most of the highways and roads on the island were closed to the public. Only one road was closed (undisclosed, but likely one leading to Mitchel Field), authorities announced, and traveling on the island was about as possible as ever. It was also incorrectly assumed that one could no longer reach Montauk Point because it had been supposedly turned into a military installation; this, too, was untrue. Rumors were also circulating that parks and beaches would not be open during the summer of '42, the fear being that a major attack via the Atlantic Ocean could take place. No such plans were in the works as yet.[135]

Another rumor making the rounds was that a fair number of people were moving back to New York City from Long Island due to the shortage of gasoline and tires. It was true that some from the surrounding counties of the city had made or were planning such a move for that very reason, but the numbers were too small to consider it a trend. More bus lines had been added around the island to help people get where they needed to go (especially defense workers to their factory jobs). Bus routes also connected with LIRR stations so that commuters did not have to drive to Manhattan or Brooklyn.[136]

Women "trainmen" with their instructor in 1943. Women replaced many male LIRR employees during the war. "*Long Island Railroad women trainmen, back from their first run, escorting one of their instructors, Brakeman I.C. Potter, who carries flagcase and lanterns, termed 'jewelry' by railroaders.*"

As new home construction became increasingly problematic because of a lack of materials, the FHA along with local real estate people and builders began to think about converting larger existing houses to multifamily rentals. There were thousands of such homes in Nassau and Suffolk, many of them built during the late 1920s land boom. A good number of them had side as well as front entrances, making them ideal for two, three or even four families to reside in should more defense workers be needed during the war. Convincing the owners of these properties to allow the houses to be remodeled (split into units) represented quite a challenge, officials admitted, but local banks and civic organizations believed they could possibly pull it off if necessary.[137]

Although Long Island officials were doing all they could to dispel reports that the stretch of land sticking out into the ocean had not been transformed into a one-hundred-mile-long military base, the army believed the island was vulnerable to attack. In May 1942, two new battalions of the New York Guard (a state volunteer force that assisted the National Guard) were created by Governor Lehman for duty in Nassau and Suffolk Counties. The battalions (consisting of local citizens) could warn of an enemy approach and slow an attack until army troops arrived, the thinking went, as the island's lengthy coasts were viewed as ideal landing areas for boats. (Bootleggers thought similarly during Prohibition.) Guard members would be stationed near where they lived, the designated towns being Freeport, Farmingdale, Patchogue, Bayshore, Riverhead, Quogue, Southampton and Greenport.[138]

A female ticket taker on a LIRR train in 1943. *"Miss Mildred L. Bunel, Long Island Railroad woman trainmen consulting a timetable for a passenger."*

The idea that Nazi saboteurs would arrive on a Long Island beach may have seemed farfetched, but that is exactly what happened just a couple weeks after the call for more Coast Guard members. Four German sailors (two in bathing suits) waded ashore on a foggy night in June, while another foursome did the same near Jacksonville, Florida. Twenty-one-year-old John C. Cullen, a coastguardsman on patrol, spotted the sailors who landed on the beach at Amagansett, and he pretended to accept their $300 bribe to "forget it." (The Nazis shortchanged him by $40, Cullen later explained, adding that he believed their leader tried to hypnotize him.) The four men claimed to be clammers from Southampton who had run aground, but Cullen knew that there were no clams in that area. He notified his superiors about the men (one of whom spoke in German), and they were found and arrested by the FBI (on orders from J. Edgar Hoover himself). The Nazis were soon tried for espionage, sabotage and conspiracy, and Cullen was promoted to the rank of coxswain for his actions.[139]

Now that it was known that there were German submarines off the coast and that it was possible for the enemy to reach the shore, all kinds of boats and ships were put in service as the Coast Guard Temporary Reserve. Like the New York Coast Guard, the Temporary Reserve consisted of volunteers of all social and economic backgrounds; oystermen, wealthy yachtsmen, and young college grads made up a typical crew. Any vessel considered seaworthy was welcome. Most had until recently been pleasure crafts, with quite a few world-class yachts part of the fleet. Beautiful sailboats that had raced in Bermuda were now painted in Coast Guard gray and used to search the waters off Long Island for any sign of unusual activity. Some modifications to the crafts were always required, and their owners had to relinquish control to the Coast Guard (and cancel their insurance).[140]

An equivalent effort being made was the ongoing search of the skies for enemy aircraft. With many planes flying over Long Island in 1942, it was perhaps not too surprising for two of them to meet in midair. It would be two army fighter planes that collided six thousand feet over Islip Terrace, although the fate of each pilot would be very different. The single-seater fighter flown by Lieutenant Lyman Rhodes was literally torn in two pieces when struck by the plane piloted by Captain Philip Tukey. Rhodes, a twenty-three-year-old from Baton Rouge, was trapped in the forward section of his plane when it crashed at Fernwood Boulevard and Hemlock Avenue. He burned to death in the cockpit, which had landed upside down. The tail section of the plane landed about a quarter mile away in a clump of trees south of Sunrise Highway. Incredibly, Tukey's fighter, with holes in its wings and a badly vibrating propeller, was able to glide the twenty miles back to Mitchel Field, where it landed safely. The captain from Maine was not hurt; neither was anyone on the ground.[141]

DANGEROUSLY LOW

Protecting the nation from invaders by land, sea and air was just part of Long Islanders' war effort. Contributions and sacrifices were being made in all kinds of ways, entirely typical of what was taking place across the country in the early 1940s. Some of the island's wealthier families were loaning out their big estates for use as medical, rest and recreational centers for servicemen, with some front lawns turned into victory gardens. Other repurposing of estates was taking place as well. Walter P. Chrysler's spread at King's Point in Great Neck was converted into a maritime training academy (the "Annapolis of the Merchant Marine" would be dedicated in September 1943), and Monhannes (the Kermit Roosevelt estate at Cove Neck in Oyster Bay) became a convalescent home for merchant seamen. By early 1943, the refugee children had left Mrs. Guggenheim's estate in Sand's Point, but the rich woman remained in a small cottage on the grounds while the castle was used as an aeronautical research laboratory.[142]

Meanwhile, almost five hundred men were moving into the one-hundred-room French-style chateau near Huntington that had belonged to Otto H. Kahn, the investment banker (and so-called King of New York). The 445-acre estate (which had a few years earlier been used as a recreation center for New York City garbagemen) was now a maritime service training school, with no shortage of space for classrooms and living quarters. An indoor (marble and tile) swimming pool, formal gardens with fountains, museum-quality statuary and a fifteen-foot hedge of sycamore trees were part of the campus now intended to produce three thousand radio operators a year (making about sixty dollars a month).[143]

Not to be outdone, the Army Signal Corps soon snagged the Clarence Mackay estate at Harbor Hill near Roslyn, which had been for sale since

1939. This estate (which had been a wedding present) covered 506 acres, and while most of Mackay's collection of art and armor had been removed by then, valuable statues remained on the grounds (which included three farms as well as greenhouses and stables). Mackay had entertained the likes of the Prince of Wales and Charles Lindbergh in the main house, designed by Stanford White in the French Gothic style; its enormous great hall had been brought in from an ancient cathedral in Burgundy. Now, however, Harbor Hill was surrounded by Hempstead Turnpike, Glen Cove Avenue, Red Ground Road, the LIRR and Roslyn High School, making it a vestige of another age.[144]

Next to go (for one dollar in rent a year) was the 1,700-acre Marshall Field estate at Lloyd Neck near Huntington, which was turned into what the Office of War Information (OWI) called a "technical training center." The school was actually for students to learn the art of overseas propaganda, with classes in leaflet writing, microphone techniques and intelligence gathering. Former journalists, radio technicians, cartoonists and college professors were taking subjects ranging from "sociological studies of enemy nations" to "methods of balking physical assaults" to "how to operate effectively without divulging your movements or activities to the enemy." Just three hundred acres of the estate was required for such training on what was believed to be the longest stretch of privately owned waterfront on Long Island. The driveway alone was two miles long, but the view from the sixty-five-room Georgian house on Long Island Sound was well worth the trip. The paintings in the house had been replaced by OWI posters, strategic charts and maps of the world's battlefronts, and the front lawn was being used for physical training.[145]

With golf memberships seriously depleted during the war as men enlisted, Long Island country clubs also had lots of land and facilities going largely unused. One was Glen Oaks and Country Club near Great Neck, which the army decided would be a good place to set up shop. (Nearby Albans Country Cub in Queens had recently been taken over by the navy for use as a hospital.) The remaining golfers from Glen Oaks moved down the road a bit to the Lakeville Club in Lake Success, which now would be known as Glen Oaks. The members of Glen Oaks had already contributed substantially to the war effort by giving money to the Red Cross and the USO, as well as subscribing to more than $1 million in bonds, but giving up their beloved golf course was for them quite the sacrifice.[146]

Long Island women (and girls) were doing their part, of course, with some of them honored for this in March 1943 at the Hempstead Golf

Club. Merian Schulze of Hempstead was raising pigeons for military work; Mildred Brittingham of Freeport was a sheet metal worker; Hope and Gloria Decker were schoolgirls who had sold many war bonds; Mary Eldridge of Franklin Square was a policewoman in a war plant; Beatrice Joyce of Lawrence was part of the Auxiliary Aircraft Warning Service; Anna Beckvar of Valley Stream built military radios; Fay Gershon of Glen Cove was in the American Women's Voluntary Services; Theresa Tobin of New Hyde Park was in the Red Cross; and Lieutenant Helen Summers of Mitchel Field was an army nurse. Each honoree received a war bond for her service.[147]

Young women from the city were also contributing to the war effort but doing it on Long Island. One hundred female students from Hunter, Queens, Barnard and other colleges spent their summer of 1943 helping Farmingdale-area vegetable growers cultivate and weed their land and, later, harvest the crops. The farmers could certainly have used the help, as much of their labor force had joined up, and New York City relied on Long Island crops for part of its food supply.[148] No fewer than eight thousand girls and boys from New York City and Long Island visited Mitchel Field in June for a tour of the airbase, which included real-life fighter and bomber planes like the Flying Fortress, Liberator and Thunderbolt. A staged battle between American and Nazi soldiers was also part of the exciting day, with the outcome of the fight never in doubt.[149]

While much had changed on Long Island over the past couple of years, much else stayed the same. The state parks, including Jones Beach, remained open, although some facilities were not operating and everything shut down at dark.[150] Mobilization drills, simulated attacks and occasional surprise blackouts across the island were other reminders that we were a nation at war. It was in the Hamptons, however, where time seemed most to have stood still. House rentals for the summer were as busy as ever, and inns such as the Sea Spray, Maidstone Arms, the Huntting, the Georgia Beach Cottage and the Hedges were fully booked. With the gasoline shortage, people were getting around on buses, bicycles and sailboats, a minor inconvenience. And while the Maidstone Club had suspended dinner, evening parties and formal entertainment for the duration, there was golf, tennis and luncheon to enjoy, during which one could almost forget there was a war going on.[151]

Alongside the good times, however, both all-year and seasonal Hamptonites were backing the attack. For those who wanted to donate blood, the local Red Cross headquarters was in a house on Main Street in East Hampton, kindly donated by the Seaburys, and there was a Service Men's Club (similar to a USO canteen) for soldiers, sailors and Coasties nearby. More than four hundred locals had reportedly joined the armed forces, and some of them had already perished in the fighting overseas.[152] Things were also hopping in Westhampton Beach that summer, with a USO golf tournament at the country club.[153]

Hopefully, Hamptonites enjoyed other beverages than beer, which was in short supply on Long Island for much of the war. Brewers were reluctant to use much of their gasoline to deliver the stuff in trucks out to Nassau and Suffolk, knowing it was more efficient to prioritize bars and grills in denser New York City. Long Island hoteliers and restauranteurs weren't happy about being cut off, especially given the fact that many of the thousands of service personnel stationed on the island enjoyed a pint of beer now and then. Peter Katavalos, owner of the Court View Hotel in Mineola and president of the Nassau County Hotel and Restaurant Association, complained to the Brewers' Board of Trade in Manhattan, telling the group that beer supplies in Nassau were "dangerously low." Most concerning, he said, the soldiers and sailors would drink hard liquor if beer wasn't available, that in itself posing a potentially dangerous situation.[154]

While a glass of beer was difficult to find on Long Island, there was plenty of duck. The island was famous for its ducklings, of course, and the war appeared to have little impact on how many reached the market. In one week alone in May 1944, about 750,000 pounds (or 41,000 barrels) of duckling was delivered to food merchants in New York City. That was good news given the shortage of spring chickens (as well as beef and lamb), and many housewives found themselves serving meals like duck a l'orange to their families for the first time.[155]

Atoms for Peace

By the spring of 1944, with the war turning decidedly in the favor of the Allies, some wartime restrictions on Long Island were beginning to relax. Many anglers were glad to hear that the Coast Guard had lifted its two-year-old ban on offshore fishing, although charter fishing boats and private pleasure craft were still not allowed in the newly opened waters about five miles off the coast. While that was good news for fisherman in Freeport, Lindenhurst, Babylon, Bay Shore, Canoe Place and Montauk Harbor, many of them no longer had boats, having turned them over to the Coast Guard or seen them converted for commercial fishing. Without a boat with which to fish, captains had taken other jobs, and it was uncertain whether they would return to the sea. As well, gasoline shortages remained, further incentive to choose an occupation that did not require fuel. Some fishermen were no doubt unhappy about being turned into landlubbers, especially given the reports that mackerel was abundant and soon there would be plenty of bonita, albacore, sea bass, fluke, blackfish and porgies swimming in the local waters.[156]

With the war's end in September 1945, however, many Long Island fishermen would soon be able to return to their boats if they chose to do so. Real estate developers, too, were going back to what they had done before the war, despite it being difficult or impossible to build a house. In November, for example, hundreds of acres of farmland in Jericho, Westbury and Bethpage were sold to home builders, the beginnings of what would become yet another boom in Long Island real estate. It was surprising that so much land could still be found on the island, but the purchases showed that large tracts remained.[157] While developers were ready to go, a persistent shortage of construction materials put the brakes on their eagerness to be fully back in business. About one thousand homes were in some stage of completion in Nassau County at year-end 1945, but they couldn't be finished until things like water heaters were produced and made available.[158]

Highway projects, too, turned on like a faucet right after V-J Day, and there was no material shortage to slow them down. A new nine-mile extension of the Northern State Parkway near Hicksville had already begun, with a new gas station to be built along it on the Nassau-Suffolk line. There was still a labor shortage as soldiers and sailors transitioned back to civilian life, but new giant mechanical equipment was helping get the job done. Considerable progress had been made during the war with regard to earth-moving equipment (airports had to be created in many places from scratch), and these machines were finding ideal applications in peacetime.[159] Naturally, Robert Moses had many plans for both the parkways and state parks on Long Island, and he made them public in early 1946. Moses had had four years to think about what he wanted to do, coming up with a budget of $22 million ($19 million for parkway construction, $2 million for improvements to Jones Beach and $1 million for improvements to the other state parks).[160]

Rather unexpectedly, there was another significant postwar development on Long Island: the arrival of the United Nations to Lake Success. In just slightly more than a year, the UN had taken a nomadic route, moving from San Francisco to London to Hunter College's campus in the Bronx. In

August 1946, the international peacekeeping organization set up shop in the headquarters of the Sperry Gyroscope Company in Lake Success. Even this move was planned to be temporary, however, with a permanent home to be built somewhere over the next three to five years, probably in Westchester County in New York or Fairfield County in Connecticut.[161]

As it turned out, the UN Security Council would hold its day-to-day activities in Lake Success for almost five years, after which it moved to its new headquarters on the East Side of Manhattan in May 1951. (The UN General Assembly met in what had been the New York City Building on the fairgrounds in Flushing Meadows.) Citizens of Lake Success actually got to vote on whether they wanted the organization in their town, with 118 yeas and 70 nays. Tourists could and frequently did visit the headquarters, and much excitement surrounded Eleanor Roosevelt's occasional appearance.[162]

Farther out on the island, world peace was being sought but in quite a different way. (A good thing, given that talks at the UN's Atomic Energy Commission had stalled.) Work had begun at Brookhaven National Laboratory, a vast new nuclear research center intended to harness the power of atomic energy for the benefit of mankind. This was the "first atomic project devoted solely to peace," according to Kenneth Bilby of the *New York Herald Tribune*, meaning the nuclear reactor would be used in medicine, physics, biology, chemistry and engineering. This was a prime example of "atoms for peace"—i.e., the postwar vision of using atomic energy for constructive versus destructive purposes. To that point, unlike the secrecy that surrounded Oak Ridge and Los Alamos, where the atomic bombs used by the United States against Japan had been developed, Brookhaven's scientists and administrative employees along with their families watched as the ground was broken for the lab in Brookhaven. Five hundred spectators cheered as the land for the six-story building was cleared on what had been the army's Camp Upton.[163]

While improving international relations was top of mind for some Long Islanders, tourism had rebounded nicely after the war, as city people again flocked to the island for its extraordinary scenic beauty and recreational activities. There were boating, fishing, hundreds of miles of bridle paths and no fewer than one hundred golf courses for those who had some time and money to spend. Swimming in sheltered bays or surfing—a sport that was gaining in popularity, in part from service personnel having observed it while stationed in Hawaii—were other pleasures that drew urbanites east in warmer weather. One could rent a sailboat for the bays or charter a

A 1978 demonstration by Dr. Walter Kato of the Brookhaven National Laboratory. *Gotfryd, Bernard, photographer. "Dr. Walter Kato, Brookhaven simulator lab."*

powerboat for an ocean trip to try to land some weakfish, tuna, blues (bays) or striped bass (ocean) or just enjoy the ride. More daring anglers hunted sharks, although hiring a pro was highly recommended for that sport.[164]

Vacationers had better have brought a considerable amount of cash with them if they intended to stay a while in the most luxurious accommodations, especially in the summer, when rates shot up. Prices had gone up after the war due to inflation and as those in hospitality tried to make up some of the business they had lost the last few years. On the more desirable east end (i.e., Montauk, Shelter Island, Sag Harbor and the Hamptons) the best hotels were charging anywhere from sixteen to twenty-four dollars per person a night. A furnished room without meals could be had for just two to five dollars a night, however, and dozens of local restaurants served reasonably priced, freshly caught seafood. Even in Westhampton, which at the time was considered the most stylish of the Hamptons, a modest furnished room could be had for three to five dollars a night, quite a bargain.[165]

The Hamptons were certainly nice, and there was something to be said for catching a lunker or playing a round of golf on a course with an ocean view, but a fair share of vacationers was entirely happy simply exploring any of the dozens of villages that had unusual names like Quogue, Speonk or

Left: A very *Jaws*-like image of a real-life shark hunter in Montauk in 1978 (three years after that Long Island–based movie was released). *Gotfryd, Bernard, photographer. "Frank Mundus, shark hunting, Montauk Point, LI. i.e. Long Island."*

Right: A 1988 photo of the art deco Sag Harbor Theater. *Margolies, John, photographer. "Sag Harbor Theater, Sag Harbor, New York."*

the Moriches. Almost all were reachable by the LIRR, and one could get to the very tip of the island from Penn Station in just over three hours. (There were twice-daily flights from Manhattan and La Guardia by seaplane for those in a hurry. Wealthy Manhattanites wanting to play a round of golf and still be able to sleep in their own bed that night were most likely to go by air.) Atlantic Beach was very popular, while the more adventurous were curious to see Fire Island, the narrow (less than half a mile wide) sand bar where everyone seemed to be a painter, writer or poet. The North Shore, too, was largely undiscovered territory for some, with towns such as Orient Point, Greenport, Setauket, Stony Brook and Northport especially attractive for those interested in the early days of the island. From Greenport, one could take a ferry to Connecticut (automobiles welcome), with the delights of New England just up the road.[166]

With new postwar money being spent on Long Island's parkway system, driving all over the island was getting easier. Twenty miles of new roadway

The Montauk Point lighthouse with its keeper and his three children in 1956. *Higgins, Roger, photographer. "Charles Schumacher and children outside their home and the lighthouse he tends/World Telegram & Sun."*

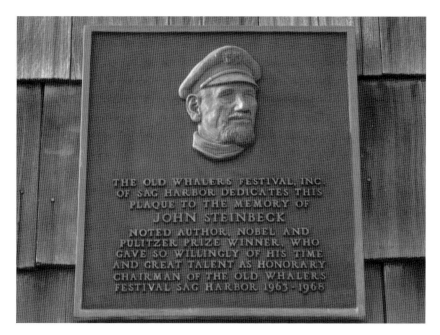

A plaque in Sag Harbor honoring the author John Steinbeck for his contributions to the Old Whaler's Festival in the 1960s. *Gotfryd, Bernard, photographer. "Steinbeck Plaque in Sag Harbor, L.I."*

An old inn in Montauk around mid-century. *The Miriam and Ira D. Wallach Division of Art, Prints and Photographs: Photography Collection, The New York Public Library. "Montauk, N.Y." New York Public Library Digital Collections.*

Downtown Montauk in the 1950s was decidedly rustic. *The Miriam and Ira D. Wallach Division of Art, Prints and Photographs: Photography Collection, The New York Public Library. "Montauk, NY." New York Public Library Digital Collections.*

A quintessential beach scene at Atlantic Beach in the summer of 1947. Women's bathing suits may be less skimpy now, but not much else has changed in three quarters of a century. *Gottscho-Schleisner, Inc., photographer. "Surf Club, Atlantic Beach, Long Island, New York. Beach scene III."*

The Fire Island lighthouse in 1952. The boy's father was the lighthouse keeper. *Higgins, Roger, photographer. "Richard Mahler 5 is the Fire Island School's youngest pupil and lives the farthest away. His father is the lighthouse keeper and, since the lighthouse is about four miles away, school is a long ride by jeep / World Telegram & Sun."*

in both Nassau and Suffolk were being added in late 1947; not just the Northern State was being extended, but additions were also being made to the Southern State, and that parkway was being made safer as well. Traffic on that road used to go around the south end of Hempstead Lake, which meant motorists encountered several dangerous curves, but now it went across the lake, promising to reduce the number of accidents.[167]

LAND RUSH

Not that far from Hempstead Lake, William Levitt and his sons were building a community that for many would come to define the American dream. Levitt had already been in the business for a couple of decades, along with others blazing the suburban trail of Long Island. ("We think Long Island is God's country," Levitt once remarked.) By 1948, his Manhasset-based firm and that of Gross-Morton had risen to the top of home building on the island. There was much snow on the ground in February that year, but Levitt's construction projects continued, their foundations having already been prepared. There were many developers on Long Island, but Levitt and Alfred Gross approached the business not unlike Henry Ford had done with automobiles. Continuous large-scale operations were the key to efficient, mass-produced building, they knew, distancing themselves from the rest of the pack and making a huge amount of money in the process.[168]

On a number of levels, Long Islander developers like Levitt and Gross had an advantage over most others in the United States. Beyond having a large continuous spillover of potential buyers from the country's most populous city just to the west, the land of Long Island was ideally suited for development. Alongside urban decentralization, there were sizable flat stretches on which to build, particularly in the center of the island, and the sandy soil made it easy for steam shovels to dig into the earth. Unlike in many other parts of the country, Long Island builders' bulldozers and trenchers effortlessly chewed up tree roots and granite ledges. Farmland was quickly turned into neatly arranged suburban landscapes, geographical or topographical confirmation that—for large-scale housing development, at least—Long Island was indeed God's country.[169]

While Levitt was about to take the business model to a new level, it had actually been Alfred Gross who pioneered the concept of "whole community" (versus individual house) development. Between the late 1920s and early 1930s, Gross built about 2,500 houses in Laurelton, Queens, to create what many agreed was the nation's largest community of moderately priced homes. The formula consisted of acquiring lots of land at reasonable prices, purchasing materials at a bulk rate, using mass production principles to build the houses and offering easy financing or credit for buyers. In 1948, Gross was using that same formula to build a 3,800-unit garden apartment community in Glen Oaks Village, Queens, while Levitt was focusing on Nassau County. In addition to taking a systematic planning approach to building, Levitt included appliances and other extras in the cost of a house, a brilliant marketing move that was said to win many housewives over.[170]

Levittown, as it was called, was initially a rental housing community designed for war veterans. Despite a record snowfall in early 1948, Levitt kept building, as demand remained strong. (He was, however, unable to keep up his thirty-houses-a-day pace.) Two thousand houses had already been built, and another four thousand were on the way, which would bring the population of the town to twenty-five thousand by the end of the year.

A house on Regent Lane in Levittown in 1958. Mrs. Robert Berman, residence at 3626 Regent Lane. *Gottscho-Schleisner, Inc., photographer. 1958 Aug. 28. Library of Congress Prints and Photographs Division, Washington, D.C.*

Houses on Winding Lane in Levittown in 1958. Homes in the classic suburban community were less cookie-cutter than popularly believed. Peg Brennan, residence at 25 Winding Lane. *Gottscho-Schleisner, Inc., photographer. 1958 Aug. 28. Library of Congress Prints and Photographs Division, Washington, D.C.*

The American Legion had formed Levittown Post 1711, which was said to already have the most members of any post in New York State and possibly the nation. Two weekly newspapers were being published, adding to the community feel of the mass-produced town.[171]

By March that year, the snow was beginning to melt, allowing Levitt to gear up to full speed, which would be six hundred houses a month (each renting for $65 per month). The numbers associated with a fully completed Levittown were staggering. The community would have more than one hundred miles of paved roads, Levitt announced, and over two hundred miles of sidewalks and curbs. Three large shopping centers were planned, the biggest to cover twenty acres along Hempstead Turnpike and the others twelve acres each north and south of the turnpike.[172] Levittown was well on the way to becoming the country's largest single postwar housing development and biggest rental project ever undertaken.[173]

Levitt was hardly done making his town bigger and better, however. There would be six swimming pools (one for each thousand families) as part of a new park district to be built, he revealed in August 1948, all at no additional charge to residents.[174] A week later, Levitt had more news: his firm had purchased an additional adjoining five hundred acres of land, which would enable two thousand more houses to be built. Levittown would consist of eight thousand houses by the end of 1949, he told the media, although these two thousand new houses would be for sale rather than rent. With this addition, the population of Levittown would be thirty-two thousand, placing it among the largest localities on Long Island.[175]

Levitt soon made national news, but it was regarding his Strathmore development in Manhasset. Over a weekend in October, *Newsweek* magazine reported, Long Island highways were jammed with people wanting to take a look at the development. Hundreds had brought cash along and offered to buy a yet-to-be built house in the community. Levitt hadn't advertised at all, yet swarms of people were interested in one of the $18,500–$24,000 houses (which really did include the proverbial suburban two-car garage). Levitt's Strathmore was indeed a "fast-selling dream," as *Newsweek* referred to it, but it was his Levittown that was making history.[176] In December 1948, the six-thousandth tenant moved into the community that sat on a former one-thousand-acre potato farm, fourteen months after the first veteran (Theodore Bladykas) called Levittown home. Levitt & Sons had invested $50 million in the town that bore their name, a lot of money by any measure.[177] *Time* magazine thought Levittown, with its lookalike houses, had "a barracks-like air" (Levitt had built wartime housing), but residents didn't mind or actually preferred the cookie-cutter style (perhaps a function of their having served in the military).[178]

Time described the mass pursuit of a Levittown house as a "land rush," which was exactly what took place in March 1949 when applications opened to buy one of the first 350 built. Hundreds of people stood in line at Levitt & Son's Roslyn office, some of them having spent one or even two nights camping out. The "1949 Levitt model" sold for $7,990, with a $90 down payment required at signing and $58 monthly installments to follow. Only veterans could buy the two-story houses with four finished rooms that had space in the attic for two more rooms. As usual with a Levitt house, appliances and venetian blinds were included, as was landscaping on the grounds. Incredibly, taxes, water and fire insurance were also included in the price, making it no wonder so many people wanted one.[179]

Unable to rent a Levittown house, even if they had served in the war, were African Americans (and, presumably, Asian Americans). Like

Strathmore, Levittown was redlined, as a clause in a rental prospectus for the development made clear. ("No dwelling shall be used or occupied except by members of the Caucasian race," Clause 25 read, although non-Caucasian "domestic servants" were permitted.) The FHA tried to eliminate the clause to resolve what was overt race discrimination, but the agency lacked the power to do so (even though Levittown was an FHA-backed project). In March 1949, a number of groups, including the National Association for the Advancement of Colored People (NAACP), the American Jewish Congress and the American Jewish Committee, condemned not just Levittown's rental policy but also the FHA's inability to do anything about it.[180] Two months later, however, and clearly under considerable pressure, Levitt dropped the clause from the leases. (No such clause had been in sales contracts, meaning that for a couple of months, African Americans, Asian Americans and other racial minorities could theoretically buy but not rent a Levittown house, rather oddly.)[181] Levitt still had the right to choose to whom he'd sell or rent a house, however, meaning the race issue wasn't completely resolved.[182]

By June 1949, the population of Levittown had reached thirty-three thousand—the size of a small city. Families were already using two of the planned shopping centers, with another two on the way. The recreation center, with its bowling alley meeting rooms, and snack bar, had opened, too. Schools and churches were being constructed, and the town's initially criticized bus system was getting better. The two weekly newspapers had evolved into the *Levittown Tribune*, and almost fifty organizations had been formed. By the end of the year, there would be not eight but ten thousand houses in Levittown, Levitt was now saying, many of them filled with children. A large playground had been built for them, and baby carriages could be seen everywhere in the community. It being the Automobile Age, cars, too, were a ubiquitous presence.[183]

Levittown was not yet complete, but some observers already understood some of the implications associated with it. In a front-page story for the *New York Times* that same month, Frederick Graham described what he called the "urban revolt" that was taking place as Long Island grew rapidly. The island was experiencing a boom, but this one was not the brief, up-and-down kind of an oil town or a city with wartime factories. Long Island's boom was, rather simply, about having a home, usually for the first time. Those moving to Long Island typically ranged between twenty-seven and thirty-seven years old, precisely the age when young married couples were having children and desiring material possessions.

The Levittown Center shopping center in 1957. *Higgins, Roger, photographer. "Levittown Center shopping center, Levittown, Long Island, N.Y. / World Telegram & Sun."*

A home with a yard, near good schools and in a safe neighborhood fit this sociological and economic model, even if that house was modest and sat on a small plot of land. That model was, of course, the American dream, a psychological longing for a private space made possible by high wages and full employment for White males. The hardships of the Depression and scarcity of goods during the war had intensified this dream; now it was for sale for just ninety dollars down.[184]

Was the postwar American dream playing out in Long Island perfect? Hardly. Already, the pressures of population growth (at a much higher rate than New York City, New York State and the nation) were starting to show. Much of Nassau and Suffolk Counties was a massive construction zone, not a particularly attractive sight. Trees were scarce and small (like those in Garden City had been decades earlier before they multiplied and grew), and hundreds of retailers and light industrial manufacturers had sprung up seemingly overnight. Utilities were being strained, and everyday life was essentially impossible without owning an automobile. The demand and supply for an alternative to urbanism were unrelenting, however. In July 1949, another builder, Harry Leibowitz, bought thirty acres near Levittown on the east side of the Massapequa-Hicksville Road that he planned to develop into 1,200 single-family dwellings.[185]

Would all of Long Island be transformed into neatly arranged boxes in designed communities, making the island somewhat less than "God's country"? Civic leaders were fully aware that their communities were suffering growing pains but were unsure how to manage the inevitable future expansion.[186] America and Long Island were about to enter the second half of the twentieth century, however, with a host of new and unanticipated challenges waiting to unfold.

Chapter 4

A LILY-WHITE COMMUNITY

The future pattern of urban living throughout the nation is being foreshadowed in large measure by the Levittown type of community.
—Richard B. Lyman, 1953

O n a Thursday evening in April 1951, a group of people gathered at the Mid-Island Inn on the South Village Green in Levittown, Long Island. The event was billed as a "lawn-making rally," with a trio of authorities on the subject invited to instruct new homeowners in the art and science of growing grass and other flora. An agronomist gave a talk on how to make a new lawn or renovate an existing one, after which a soil expert explained how to use a sedge-peat humus to improve root growth. Finally, a specialist in agricultural chemicals showed a color film called *How Does Your Garden Grow?*, with narration by none other than Lowell Thomas, the well-known peripatetic journalist. Admission was free, and door prizes were given to those holding the lucky numbers.[187]

Such were some of the leisure activities on the crabgrass frontier in midcentury America. Long Island in the 1950s was, on the surface, an idyllic place, especially for the many families wanting their share of the American dream after the turbulent Depression and war years. Homes with white picket fences were indeed popping up all over Nassau and Suffolk Counties, filled with working dads, housewives and a few kids who would one day be known as baby boomers. Levittown was the archetypical suburban town, setting the standard for thousands of other communities that flourished through the postwar years. For some, however, this Norman Rockwellian image was far from reality, as America's racial prejudices made themselves readily apparent.

THE PRESS OF THE CITY

Now firmly established, the monster community that had been plopped down in the middle of Long Island began to resemble towns that had existed for decades or centuries. Bill Levitt had planted the seeds in what had been a potato field, but now it was the (all-White) residents of Levittown who were making their community blossom. Unlike African Americans and Asian Americans, Jews were allowed to rent and buy houses there (Levitt was himself Jewish), and some Jewish residents struck an interesting bargain with their Christian neighbors. A member of a Christian family would babysit for a Jewish family on Friday nights so the latter could attend religious services, and vice versa on Sunday mornings to allow the former to go to church. More than one hundred families had signed up for the experimental exchange program, in which neighbors who lived close to each other would pair off. It was hoped that the swap would have a ripple effect throughout the community by bringing Jews and Christians, who tended not to mingle much, closer together. (Another strategy to achieve that same goal was the reading of both the Hanukkah and Christmas stories in young students' classes in Levittown's three schools during the holidays.)[188]

Retail growth soon followed residential development, especially in the consumption-oriented suburbs, and that was the case for Levittown. By early 1950, a huge shopping area (the equivalent of fourteen city blocks) called Levittown Center was rising, it too on what had been farmland. The thirty-acre tract located on a corner of Hempstead Turnpike would soon be the site of one of the biggest retail centers on the East Coast. Not only was there going to be both a Grand Union and an A&P supermarket and many other stores and services, but parents would also be able to leave their children in a nursery while they shopped (at no cost). Parking space for 2,500 automobiles was also part of the development.[189]

With that piece of the puzzle added, Levitt felt there was yet more room for growth, and his company soon bought another 1,200 acres to allow him to extend his titular town. With that purchase of what had been no fewer than thirty old farm sites, Levittown could reach into the Oyster Bay

Township (the community had until then been contained to the township of Hempstead). The acquisition was one of the largest residential realty deals ever made on Long Island and made it clear that experts believed strong demand remained for one-family homes on the island for the White middle-class.[190]

Such experts were keen on continued development on Long Island for a number of reasons, the primary one being that land was cheaper there than in other suburbs of New York City. The decentralization of the city's population was moving down the economic and social scale, data showed, meaning Long Island was at an advantage over Westchester, northern New Jersey and Fairfield County in Connecticut. Expanding Manhattan- and Brooklyn-based businesses were theoretically more likely to choose Long Island to set up shop, as both space for the companies and housing for their employees would cost less there than in other suburban communities. Commuters who made less money (i.e., the lower middle class) would also find Long Island more attractive than surrounding areas. "It is the people of smaller incomes who are now most actively seeking to get their families into living zones outside of the press of the city," said Burke Harmon, whose company had completed a survey on population trends in New York City's suburbs. "Long Island is more favorably located than any other commuting area for the majority of these people," the LIRR's spotty service (and occasional fatal crash) notwithstanding.[191]

Builders also recognized that a more price-sensitive market was emerging on Long Island at mid-century. More housing for families with household incomes of $3,000–$5,000 was needed, according to Leonard Frank of the Long Island Home Builders Institute, making Suffolk County the logical choice for development. Lending institutions were following suit by offering mortgages for buyers of low-cost homes and spreading them out for fifteen years, making the monthly payments very affordable (about thirty-five dollars in many cases, rather incredibly). Owning one's home free and clear in fifteen years was a principal piece of the American dream for many of these folks, although redlining remained a major problem. Some developers, however, saw an opportunity to bypass the race-based qualifications for homeownership practiced by Levitt and others. The one thousand houses at Thomas Romano's 147-acre Romek Park in North Amityville, for example, were available to buyers "regardless of race, creed or color," assuming they qualified for the $7,000 homes.[192]

With easy credit to be had and "White flight" from the city ramping up, home colonies, as they were sometimes called, were springing up across

Long Island, including in towns such as Baldwin, Albertson and Merrick. In Bethpage, new houses were appearing on what had been the Skippa farm, originally owned by early Long Island settlers. The $9,000 houses there were quite deluxe; each had a large plot, a garage, an "expansion" attic, a fireplace and not just an electric range and refrigerator but also a washing machine. In Baldwin, veterans could have a $9,400 home complete with a picture window, two patios and a kitchen-dinette combination with no down payment at all.[193] One thousand homes were under construction in the 250-acre Forest City development in Wantagh, which was formerly the Ogden Phipps game preserve.[194]

While William Levitt was the reigning king of Long Island residential real estate development, the vigorous building activity showed that he was in competition with dozens of other speculators and syndicates offering buyers similarly attractive packages. In March 1950, Levitt announced that there would be four movie theaters in Levittown (population now forty thousand), complementing the extensive shopping facilities. Levitt envisioned that eighty thousand people would one day call Levittown home, another reason to add amenities. The five-hundred-seat theaters would be of identical design, not surprisingly, and "emphasize the homey and informal character rather than the lush and glittering atmosphere of the big city," he explained.[195]

Almost all builders had a model home for potential buyers to inspect, with crowds often doing just that every Sunday. For his "1950 model" houses, however, Levitt outdid himself, creating an exhibit center to display not just the models—actually two, one traditional and one modern—but their materials and how they were constructed. One of Levittown's eight swimming pools was conveniently located right behind the world's fair–style exhibit, further tempting house shoppers considering other developments. The new model would also include a built-in television set, and Levitt was matching the no-down-payment-necessary offer for military vets.[196]

Levitt's promotion for his "1950 model" seemed to do the trick. One thousand more houses than planned were somehow squeezed into the community, bringing the number up from four to five thousand. The more luxurious houses Levitt built at the Roslyn Country Club had also sold out; those four hundred homes were priced at an average $20,000 apiece. Because of the Korean War, however, Levitt and other builders believed that fewer houses would be built in 1951, justification for putting potential buyers on a waiting list.[197]

The 1950 census made it clear why real estate developers were selling more houses than they could produce. Nassau County had 64 percent more people in 1950 than 1940, making it New York City's fastest-growing suburb. Suffolk County's population had increased an impressive 38 percent over that same period, but it was not suffering the kind of growing pains of its neighbor to the west. New schools were needed as the generation to be known as baby boomers grew up, and utilities of all kinds—water, gas, electric and sanitation—were insufficient to meet the need. Police and firefighter departments were short-staffed as well, especially because almost all of them were voluntary, some of them dating from the nineteenth century. (There were, in fact, 156 voluntary fire departments on Long Island in 1951; only Long Beach and Garden City had professionals doing the job.)[198] Taxes were being raised to pay for such necessary things, making Long Island less affordable than hoped and bringing a heavy dose of reality to the American dream.[199]

The American dream wasn't having just a home of one's own, of course, but also everything that typically went into it. Driven by the baby boom and as a reaction to the thrift of the Depression years and sacrifices during wartime, the postwar years were a golden age of consumerism, particularly in acquisition-oriented, peer-pressured suburbia. In 1950, *Architectural Forum* surveyed one hundred Levittown families to find out what they had purchased for their homes over the past year. The magazine found that the typical Levittown family had spent $1,432 (about $18,000 today) on furniture, cars, radios and TVs, nursery items, dishes, toasters, irons and electric mixers, garden equipment, lawn furniture, draperies, sewing machines and carpeting. It was a good thing that refrigerators and washing machines came with the houses, or the homeowners would have bought those too. By extrapolating the numbers, the editors of *Architectural Forum* estimated that the fifteen thousand Levittown families had collectively spent about $22 million ($270 million today) on equipping their brand-new houses over the past year, quite a windfall to the local economy.[200]

The Mass-Produced Suburbs

While Levittown represented a gold mine for Long Island retailers, it stood as a shameful reminder of the racial prejudices embedded in suburban development. In December 1950, the leases of two Levittown couples were not renewed, the alleged reason being that they had regularly allowed their children to play with the African American children who lived next door. (The Black family had somehow been able to rent a house in the generally redlined community.) The bias case went to the New York District Supreme Court in Mineola, with lawyers hired for the couples by the NAACP, American Jewish Congress and American Jewish Committee. Amazingly, Levitt's attorney didn't deny the charges, simply saying there was no law requiring his client to renew their leases.[201] The couples lost, appealed but lost that case as well, with the appellate judge ruling that there weren't facts to warrant action.[202]

The residents of Levittown, however, seemed much more empathetic and tolerant than its owner, at least in relation to Indian orphans. In May 1951, seven trucks (one of them borrowed from the local civil defense unit) cruised through the northwestern portion of the fifteen-thousand-home community collecting food for orphanages in India, which was experiencing a famine. Women block captains went door-to-door, adding to the pile of dried and canned foods, and the Levittown Junior League, a Girl Scout Troop and a unit of the Eastern Star (a fraternal organization) helped out. The organizer of the event, a Mrs. Irwin Pollock, who had contacts at the Indian embassy in Washington, got the idea for it while standing in line at the local supermarket and watching the "tremendous amounts of food passing over the checkers' counters." By end of day, three tons of food had been donated, quite a lot given that the area canvassed covered just one-sixth of Levittown.[203]

If there was any more doubt that Levittown had become a legitimate community despite being just a couple of years old, it was perhaps dispelled when its first Little League baseball game was played in August 1951. Four teams (two in the National League and two in the American League) consisting of eight- to twelve-year-olds had been formed, with games played on the league's own field on Ballpark Lane. On opening day, Abraham Levitt, father of William and founder of Levitt & Sons, threw out the first ball following a parade led by the Sayville Junior Fire Department Band. William Levitt and local businesspeople had donated the uniforms and gear, with six leagues of four teams each planned for the 1952 season. Twenty-one coaches and eighteen umpires had been signed up, numbers which rivaled those of Major League Baseball.[204]

While preteen boys hit and caught baseballs on Ballpark Lane, dozens of young children could often be found at the Levittown Kiddie Corner, the free indoor playroom created for shoppers at Levittown Center. Children aged three to seven were allowed in the room (sponsored by the mall's merchants) between nine o'clock in the morning and four thirty in the afternoon, with a time limit of ninety minutes. Three sides of the room were glass-paned, allowing mothers (and the rare father) to check up on their little one. Toys and activities were, of course, provided and the occasional squabble soon settled by the supervising "teachers."[205]

Soon, however, there would be no more first-timers in either Levittown's Little League or Kiddie Corner. In November 1951, the final house—the 17,447[th], to be exact—was sold, closing an important chapter in the history of Long Island. Levitt had decided to build another town, also called Levittown, in Bucks County, Pennsylvania, which had the wide-open spaces to do just that. Sixteen thousand houses were planned for the new Levittown, which, if that turned out to be accurate, would leave the original as the largest home-building project in the United States. The population of Long Island's Levittown had reached seventy thousand in just a couple of years, a gold rush–style boomtown that would not quickly disappear when the good times ended.[206]

As developers saw the demand and the money to be made from them, many more Levittown-style communities appeared in the United States through the 1950s. Millions of Americans called such places home, with the thinking being that a fair share of them would eventually move up from such middle-class developments to more luxurious ones as their incomes rose. Critics were not quite sure what to make of this new model of suburban housing, however, as there had never been anything quite like it.[207] After reading Harry Henderson's article "The Mass-Produced Suburbs" in *Harper's*, Richard B. Lyman of the *New York Herald Tribune* addressed this peculiar and wildly popular way of living:

> *The mass community has neither history, tradition, nor established structure, no inherited customs, institutions, socially important families, or big houses. Also, practically speaking, there are no rich or poor, and the large-scale projects started out with no older people, teenagers, in-laws, family doctors, "big shots," organizations, or local governments.*[208]

In writing his piece, Henderson had visited six such mass communities, the largest one being Levittown and the second-largest Lakewood, California (near Long Beach). Because the houses' exteriors were so similar, Henderson found, much effort was given to interior decorating to personalize them. The communities were highly social, and their commonality along social lines (class, age, race and education level) encouraged shared points of view on many subjects. Much thought to neighborhood planning had negated urban problems like traffic jams inside the communities (outside was a whole other matter), and previous apartment dwellers were still getting used to not bumping into each other while moving from room to room. (Crime also was virtually nonexistent.) The only thing William Levitt and his competitors had not carefully orchestrated was dogs, which brought a singular form of chaos to the otherwise startling sense of calm. Considering a dog the final piece of the suburban lifestyle, many new homeowners immediately acquired puppies, which soon proceeded to race across lawns and backyards, knock down children, wreck gardens, howl and bark at all hours and bite the occasional mailman or deliveryman.[209]

Henderson's piece, which relied on a social or cultural anthropological research approach somewhat reminiscent of the Lynds' Middletown studies, was truly remarkable, as the man recognized the significance of this new postwar suburban model as it was emerging. Towns and cities had historically developed gradually and relied heavily on local trade of some sort, but such instant communities did not. As well, older suburbs had ringed urban areas, but places like Levittown sprang up on open farmland, almost independent from their host cities. Most importantly, perhaps, the marketing of these houses relied on the kind of mass production and consumption formula that had been perfected in the first half of the twentieth century. A variety of powerful social and economic forces, including the baby boom, easy credit and expansion of the middle class, fueled the commodification of the suburbs, in the process changing much of everyday life in America and eventually the world. Levittown and its siblings were "a new generation's version of the 'American way,'" Henderson wrote, entirely in sync with their time and place.[210]

A NASTY DEVELOPMENT

That people of color were generally excluded from this new American way was the glaring problem associated with the nation's increasing number of mass-produced suburbs. While the Levitts' racist practices were notably abhorrent because of their brazenness, discrimination against African Americans was routine and pervasive across the United States in the 1950s, including on Long Island. Long Island would, in fact, serve as a battleground of civil rights through the '50s and '60s, as Blacks made a concerted effort to end the long and ugly history they had faced there. The KKK's public presence had mostly and thankfully receded, but discriminatory attitudes and policies remained part of the institutional framework on the island. Education was a prime site of bias, with both African American students and teachers often treated less fairly than their White counterparts. Blacks were actively trying to achieve equal opportunity in public schools (and other workplaces) in the early '50s on a national level, one logical strategy being through the courts.

In 1952, for example, one Dorothy J. Brown filed a lawsuit against the Elmont school board, charging that she had been denied appointment as a teacher because of her race. The NAACP lodged the complaint in the United States District Court, and the presiding judge decided that the case shouldn't be dismissed, as the school board had sought. Brown had been offered a teaching job back in 1949, but when the principal learned she was Black, he took her out of the candidate pool. Over the next few years, Brown applied for teaching jobs in five other school districts in Nassau County to establish a pattern of discrimination. That she did, as she was rejected in each instance (at a time when teachers were in extremely high demand).[211]

Events that recalled the heyday of the KKK in the 1920s were also taking place on Long Island in the 1950s. In 1953, fire was set not once but twice to the ranch house being built for an African American man named Clarence Wilson, who believed these were attempts to deter him from moving into the almost totally White neighborhood of Deauville Gardens in Copiague. (There was just one other Black family in the community.) Babylon town police described the first fire as "suspicious" after finding a kerosene can at the scene, and the second, just ten days later (with matches found at the scene), was more evidence that these were no accidents. Threatening letters sent to Wilson signed "KKK" left no doubt that was the case, even if it wasn't actually members of the organization that were setting the blazes.[212]

In response to the crime, Suffolk police said they would cruise by the construction site every twenty minutes to ensure there were no more fires. Still, the Central Long Island branch of the NAACP declared that they would put a twenty-four-hour guard there should the officers not fulfill that promise. Wilson and his family were, in the meantime, living in an apartment in Brooklyn while their seven-room, $16,000 house was being built by a second contractor (the first had backed out when pressured to do so by local residents). Wilson, the president of a cosmetics supply company, had initially announced that he wouldn't be intimidated by the arson, but partly due to concerns for the safety of his family, soon decided he would look elsewhere to build his dream home. The fact that his insurance policy was canceled and that his bank loans were discontinued had more to do with that wise decision.[213]

The plot of the Wilson story thickened a bit when a rumor started that it was the fire setters themselves, or perhaps their bosses, who bought the man's unfinished home. Whether or not that was true, it appeared, by all accounts, that it was the Deauville Gardens Community Association that didn't want a Black family moving in, rather than a couple of rogue KKK flunkies. The promised protection from law enforcement didn't take place—not surprisingly, given who was behind the crimes—and Wilson began a lawsuit against Suffolk County for grief and mental anguish. The events leading to the sale of his house were "a nasty development in one of the states supposed to show a liberality toward minorities," he said, while Eugene Reed of the Central Long Island Branch of the NAACP called it "a shameful victory for the forces of hate and bigotry." If there was anything good to come out of the ugly chapter, it was that Reed planned to launch a campaign against housing bias on Long Island.[214]

With many Long Island communities officially or unofficially redlined, some entrepreneurs recognized that there was an opportunity to be had. One was David Stein, a builder who believed there was a robust market for good housing at a reasonable price for minority groups. (The National Association of Home Builders agreed.) In 1955, Stein decided that much of his construction budget should go to building such homes, focusing the development in nonsegregated areas. Stein and his fellow investors acquired land in the northeast section of Freeport, which had been interracially middle class for some time. The group put up a model home a couple blocks east of Main Street, thinking there would be many buyers interested in the three-bedroom split-level house that sold for $13,540.[215] A couple of years later, a new community of what were billed as "interracial homes" was offered for sale in Westbury. Like Stein, the builders of Donbar Estates appeared to be directly challenging William Levitt's redline policies, aware, perhaps, that the real estate king of Long Island was on the wrong side of history.[216]

Besides the money to be made by speculators, making available affordable new homes for the Black middle class was seen as a means of revitalizing communities considered in decline. One might think that "slums" were a distinctly urban problem, but many authorities were concerned about their presence in the suburbs in the 1950s. Civic leaders, government officials, attorneys, economists and home builders all pondered how to "rehabilitate" neighborhoods defined as slums on Long Island, with race a clear factor in their criteria. Such experts judged Inwood and North Lawrence blighted and overcrowded, for example, the fact that the towns were predominantly African American no doubt influencing their judgement. Depreciating values of real estate in neighboring White communities appeared to be the driving force of these concerns.[217] Efforts for what might be called suburban renewal could be found in many other towns. In Glen Cove, a group calling itself Long Island Neighborhood Renewal took steps to "modernize" a four-story "tenement," something that required evicting the apartment building's 106 Black occupants. The building was a fire trap and had many other safety violations, the City of Glen Cove had decided, although the NAACP argued that it could be brought up to code rather than sold outright to the "renewal" group.[218]

City and town officials had other means to induce African Americans to choose another place to live. In Garden City Park in 1956, for example, local politicians proposed "down-zoning" an area from residential to industrial in order to stop more people from moving into the (mostly Black) neighborhood. Such rezoning would backfire by effectively destroying the existing neighborhood, a local pastor warned, and possibly turn it into the kind of slum that business leaders feared.[219]

Ironically, the not-in-my-backyard sentiment of a cross section of White Long Islanders was in contrast to that among the neighbors of the

A 1957 *Look* magazine photo of the Myers family, who had been the first African American residents of the Pennsylvania Levittown. *Brooks, Charlotte, photographer. "Image from LOOK—Job 57—titled Myers family."*

small number of African American residents of the original Levittown. It was believed that at least six Black families called Levittown home in 1957, although no one knew the exact number. (The geographic borders of Levittown itself were unclear.) While African Americans obviously represented a tiny fraction of the community, which consisted of an estimated 65,000 residents in 17,500 homes, there were reportedly no tensions or problems in terms of race. Betsy Yaller, who had served as executive director of the Committee to End Discrimination in Levittown, described relations between Black and White families as "most pleasant." Children played and went to school together regardless of their skin color, she maintained, and racial differences were no barrier to friendships among adults. In Levittown, Pennsylvania, some residents were objecting to the arrival of the Myers, an African American family, cause for Yaller to try to ease their concerns.[220] "We'd like everybody to know that Levittown does have successful integration," she told the *New York Amsterdam News*, adding that the few Black families who did live in Long Island's Levittown had homes scattered around the development rather than living in a particular section.[221]

With Levittown No. 3 in New Jersey, however, Levitt's good luck in the New York and Pennsylvania courts ran out. In 1959, Levitt was building a sixteen-thousand-home development near Burlington, New Jersey, and he publicly stated that he wouldn't sell houses to African Americans ("Negroes" at the time) there, just like at the first two Levittowns. (Green Fields Farm, another New Jersey builder, shamefully echoed Levitt.) A 1957 amendment to a New Jersey housing law barred discrimination in federally guaranteed loans, however, ruining Levitt's and Green Fields's plans. Seven Black families now lived in the Long Island Levittown and one in the Pennsylvania Levittown (having purchased their homes from White residents), but it appeared that there could many more in New Jersey given that state's progressive law.[222]

Rather unexpectedly, Levittown played a role in international politics when President Eisenhower mentioned that he wanted Soviet

A 1963 image of Roy Wilkins, who was then executive secretary of the NAACP. *Leffler, Warren K, photographer. "Interview: Roy Wilkins, Executive Secretary of the NAACP/ WKL," 1963.*

premier Nikita Khrushchev to see the new Pennsylvania development as a model "workers town." (Levitt had chosen its location primarily because it was near United States Steel's Fairless plant.) But even African American employees of that plant were not allowed to purchase homes in that Levittown, something Roy Wilkins of the NAACP pointed out as Khrushchev's trip to the United States neared. "Levittown, Pa. has become known the world over as the town where a single Negro family had to fight off a mob in order to occupy a modest home," he wrote in a telegram to Eisenhower, recommending that the president steer the Soviet leader away from any Levittowns. "Levittown in Long Island, N.Y. was built as a lily-white community," he added, thinking that the Russian would "score a telling propaganda point" should he be shown "almost any new housing anywhere in America."[223]

The New Suburbia

While regressive racism was evidently still very much alive on Long Island in the 1950s, much of the island had changed dramatically over the past few decades, particularly in Nassau County. Most startling, perhaps, was the transformation of Roosevelt Field and its surrounding area as the defense industry expanded its domain. One wouldn't recognize the place where Charles Lindbergh had set off for Paris in 1927, as the old airfield laid out on sandy flatlands became home to Cold War–era corporations selling jet engines and vending machine–sized computers to the armed forces. News in 1955 that a Macy's department store was coming to Roosevelt Field was somewhat incongruous but very welcome, given Long Islanders' penchant for shopping. (E.J. Korvette, a huge discount department store, got so crowded on Saturdays that finding a parking space often took longer than the shopping.) *Sales Management* estimated the buying power of the average Nassau County family as $8,000 (almost $90,000 today), making it no wonder that stores were jam-packed.[224]

Seeing such numbers, executives from another chain of department stores sensibly decided to have a presence on Long Island. S. Klein (actually S. Klein On the Square, after its flagship store on Union Square in Manhattan) was famous for its full range of merchandise at popular prices—so famous that when it opened a store in Newark, New Jersey, the crowds were so dense that many shoppers couldn't get the items on display. Worried that history would repeat itself on the opening day of the large store on Hempstead Turnpike in West Hempstead, managers decided to not advertise the bargains to be had. Still, day one in August 1955 attracted hordes of excited shoppers, causing a massive traffic jam in the area. The 1,500-car parking lot near the store quickly filled up after the ten o'clock opening, and shoppers (most of them women with a child or two in tow) grabbed the $1.99 skirts, $3.99 boys' jackets, $2.99 sheets and $0.39 hosiery. Trade sources believed that the new S. Klein store would gross about $15 million in its first year of business, drawing on the area's large market of young couples with growing families.[225] This store in the new Eastgate Plaza was reportedly the second-largest suburban department store in the country, a believable claim given that it would be able to serve one hundred thousand customers a day.[226]

Many of the big dollars spent on shopping came from defense company payrolls. Between 1950 and 1955, the population of Nassau County had risen 44 percent to one million, according to the Long Island Lighting Company, with much of this increase coming from defense workers and their families. Ninety-five thousand houses had been built in the county over this same period of time, lending support for the much-ballyhooed claim that Nassau was the "fastest-growing county in the United States." While the claim was debatable, it couldn't be argued that a new kind of persona had made its presence felt on Long Island due to the Cold War economic binge. Physicists, engineers and technicians of all stripes were ubiquitous figures in Nassau County in the postwar years as what were often called "thinking machines" gradually came of age. The pay was very good for someone who designed, developed or tested a guided missile or system for a long-range bomber, and the only real drawbacks were that one couldn't discuss what one did for a living with friends and even family members and, of course, have any Communist leanings.[227]

While scientists and engineers went to work at nearby defense companies, business types were likely to commute to Manhattan to their jobs by car or train. Despite all the roads that had been built over the years, getting to the city and back by automobile could be a dicey affair, leaving the LIRR as the best bad option. By the mid-'50s, the railroad had a well-deserved reputation as a rather terribly run operation with iffy schedules, dirty cars and a rough ride. Power failures during peak rush hours did little to make the LIRR more customer friendly; getting stranded for a couple of hours would understandably make commuters wish they had driven to work. It wasn't much of a surprise to anyone when the railroad went bankrupt.[228]

In 1955, however, the LIRR took major steps to clean up its act. The railroad's parent company, Pennsylvania Railroad, along with the Long Island Transit Authority, began a twelve-year rehabilitation program designed to both improve service and make money. New air-conditioned coaches were put in service, other cars modernized and dozens of stations repaired and repainted. As well, miles of roadbeds were smoothed, allowing passengers to think they were not riding a particularly unruly horse to or from work. Added trains and, miracle of miracles, an increasingly on-time schedule were icing on the cake. The ambitious plan appeared to be working; the LIRR had moved out of red ink to black, with the profits poured back into the rehab program.[229]

Day-trippers and vacationers from the city wishing to take in the island's scenic wonders were also happy to see that the LIRR was getting better. In recent years, most of the news one heard about Long Island was how it had become a sea of smallish homes for the middle class, with much less talk about its natural beauty. A train ride or car trip across the island served as a vivid reminder of how amazing the long strip of land really was, however. Despite the years of aggressive home building, great stretches of sand dunes alongside the ocean and bays remained, largely untouched by developers. There was much history to be learned, and Jones Beach State Park was enjoyable as ever. In addition to the beach and recreational activities to be had, one could see bandleader Guy Lombardo's musical spectacle *Arabian Nights* any night of the week at the Marine Theater.[230]

A booming defense industry, improved railroad and abundance of parks and beaches were all good reasons for developers to find new areas to build medium-priced houses for a still-growing middle class. For decades, the trend had been for speculators to keep pushing east away from the New York City metropolitan region where open land was more plentiful and cheaper. But now, with large tracts in Suffolk County increasingly difficult to source at a good price, a countertrend was in the works: go west. Builders who had passed over what was called "marginal meadowland" in Nassau County were taking another look, thinking solid ground might not be a requirement to put up some houses. A good chunk of the south shore of the county between Lawrence and Bellmore was not much above sea level but relatively cheap, making developers take another look at the area.[231]

Another reason driving this decision was that the Long Island suburbs had spread so far east that many would-be commuters were concluding they would be living too far from their jobs in the city. Indeed, developers were now finding that most buyers in Suffolk were families whose breadwinners worked on the island. That was additional rationale for investors to put their money in marginal meadowland like that which could be had in sections of Baldwin. A community called Oakwood had sprung up there in 1957 on land that cost about $15,000 an acre rather than the usual $23,000. That represented a savings on each plot of about $1,500, which could be passed on to buyers without eating into developers' standard profit. While dredging and filling the watery land was an extra expense, there was still decent money to be made if a sizable tract could be had. A bonus was that there was abundant waterfront property in marginal meadowlands like Lawrence Bay Park, as well as plenty of canals for boat owners.[232]

While some builders scoured Long Island for land to develop on the cheap, others were going the other way. Low-cost housing, spearheaded by Levitt & Sons, had been the mainstay of Long Island residential real estate after World War II, but that was beginning to change in the late 1950s. Homes in the $25,000–$35,000 price range were becoming increasingly popular, a far cry from the $7,000 models first sold in Levittown. Building fewer but more expensive houses was now more the norm than stamping out cookie-cutter homes for the masses, in part because it saved time in getting plans approved by local authorities. As well, Veterans Affairs loans had pretty much dried up by 1957, meaning current home buyers skewed wealthier than those soon after the war.[233]

Buyers were willing to fork out big bucks for more expensive homes, but they wanted something in return: customization. Future owners were more often handing builders specifications to follow, not wanting their dwelling to look like hundreds of others. As well, this more sophisticated home buyer wanted to live in an older, established town rather than an instant community, prompting developers to find vacant lots on which to build rather than large tracts. Such buyers tended to be second or third homeowners, quite a different market than the young couple realizing their dream of owning their own little piece of America.[234]

FERTILIZER AND FINISHED BASEMENTS

The evolution of residential real estate on Long Island prompted critics to reflect on the community that had really led the way in postwar housing development on the island. By 1957, it had been ten years since bulldozers began to turn the potato patches into plots, an appropriate time to consider how the area had evolved. The small farming settlement once called Island Trees had, over a decade, become perhaps the fastest-growing community in the United States, with eighty-two thousand people now said to live in the first Levittown (more than Atlantic City, New Jersey). With his system of mass production, Levitt had deservedly become known as the "Henry Ford of the building industry" (even more fitting given Ford's anti-Semitism and Levitt's racism). Over time, Levitt had moved away from renting houses to veterans (with an option to buy) to selling homes to White middle-class families, taking full advantage of the social and economic changes taking place in America. Levittown eventually grew to cover 7.3 square miles and spill over into Hicksville, Wantagh, Plainview, East Meadow and Seaford. Even more amazing, perhaps, was that more than half of its residents in 1957 were under the age of seventeen, making it a truly child-oriented community.[235]

Interestingly, the typical Levittown household circa 1957—a thirty-four-year-old veteran, his wife and their two young children—was much like those of the first settlers a decade earlier. Renters from New York City remained the primary home buyers, with the father still commuting to his white-collar job in Manhattan. Commuting was considered a less-than-joyful experience, but having a house in Levittown was well worth the time on a train or in the car. A new high school was opening up in 1957, good news as more children entered their teens. And despite popular belief among outsiders, the houses in the community were not about to fall down; while built quickly (150 a day at one point), the homes were still very much standing and would likely remain so for at least another couple of decades. In fact, a hurricane had swept across Long Island some years back, and no houses experienced major damage.[236]

Other negative perceptions about Levittown persisted, perhaps because the community deviated so greatly from the traditional path of development. Many believed Levittown would one day become a "slum" as aging houses lost their value. As yet, there was no basis for this prediction, as the average original house had increased 30 percent in value. As well, many Levittowners had improved or expanded their abodes, adding to their current market value. (The fact that all original homeowners were veterans, middle class and White served as additional evidence that the community was not a future slum, a Yale sociologist concluded.) Also contrary to prevailing thought, Levittowners did not routinely walk into the wrong house because they all looked the same. While they indeed had identical or similar floor plans, builders purposely used different exterior colors, contrasted the roof lines, arranged the windows in alternative patterns and set the houses at varying distances from the street to make them distinguishable from each other. Later remodeling and much landscaping made the houses yet more distinct, and besides that, was anyone concerned that GM and Ford made millions of the same model?[237]

While Levittown had not changed appreciably in the past ten years despite extensive home improvements, its surrounding area had. Shopping in the area had been limited in the early days of the community, but that changed as more and more retailers moved in to seize the commercial opportunities. Levittown Center and then Eastgate Plaza were doing much to supplant Hempstead as the shopping hub of Nassau County, thereby further shifting the economic epicenter of Long Island. As well, the appearance of such large shopping centers allowed Levittowners many more local job opportunities, lessening the need to commute to and from the city. More local businesses meant—in theory, at least—more tax revenues, something of considerable importance to residents across the island.[238]

Beyond the greater opportunities to spend one's money, the staples of any community had significantly expanded in Levittown since 1947. A Quonset hut initially served as the school building, but a decade later, there were modern—if overcrowded—schools, and Catholics, Protestants and Jews now had their own places of worship. (The Yale study found that residents were 45 percent Catholic, 36 percent Protestant and 17 percent Jewish.) Adult education proved surprisingly popular, so there were many courses to be had for minimal expense. (Painting from live models was the favorite, with attic construction second and auto mechanics third.) Levittown now had a choral society, opera guild, forty-four-thousand-book library and more Little League baseball players than any other community in the country. Boy Scouts, Girl Scouts, 4-H Clubs and the Police Athletic League were also active groups for the town's fifty thousand (!) kids.[239]

Was Levittown perfect? Of course not. Traffic, much of it near the schools, had become a major and potentially dangerous nuisance, and the huge department stores tended to dominate the broader landscape. Dogs doing their business on neighbors' lawns was a common complaint, as was the feeling that the LIRR charged too much for its commuting fare. And with "juvenile delinquency" considered a serious problem in the 1950s, some adults worried that there weren't enough evening activities for teens and that their kids would eventually get into some kind of trouble. (Crime within the community remained almost nonexistent.) More concerning, perhaps, was that most Levittowners did not feel a strong sense of community, as reported by the Citizens' Committee after polling residents. This was not a surprising thing given how fragmented Levittown was because of its sheer size; the place was divided into two townships, four postal districts, several voting districts, three water districts and four fire districts. As well, many homeowners viewed Levittown as just a step to bigger and better things.

Just as the Levitts had believed, many families planned to leave when their household income grew or when they ran out of space. Still, 94 percent of Levittown residents said in the poll that they would recommend it to their friends, quite a compliment.[240]

Of course, it wasn't just Levittown that brought New Yorkers to Long Island over the past decade. The city's surrounding suburbs were collectively growing faster than ever, while the boroughs of Manhattan, Brooklyn and the Bronx had stopped growing in population. (Both Queens and Staten Island were often viewed as quasi-suburbs.) While other counties in New York and in Connecticut and New Jersey had grown, the population gains between 1950 and 1957 in Nassau (75 percent) and Suffolk (92 percent) were nothing short of spectacular. Demographers predicted that the suburbs of New York City would continue to grow while the population of the city itself would stay flat—if true, a case of the tail wagging the dog.[241]

A 1958 mail survey by the magazine *Today's Living* revealed interesting insights about how new residents of three major New York City suburbs—Westchester, New Jersey and Long Island—felt about where they had chosen to live. Of New Jerseyites surveyed, 87 percent said they had friendly neighbors, with those from Westchester coming in second at 85 percent and Long Islanders third at 82 percent. And while just 1 percent of New Jersey and Westchester newcomers considered their neighbors "aggressive," 5 percent of freshly arrived Long Islanders did, a bit disturbing.[242]

Judging from this survey at least, Long Islanders were a fickle bunch. Men tended to help each other with projects, and women frequently had coffee together but nosy neighbors, "back-fence gossip" and petty quarrels were common. Long Islanders complained most about overcrowded schools, were least satisfied with the playgrounds and gave the lowest ratings for cultural activities. "It's amazing to me that intellectual activity out here centers around fertilizer and finished basements," a Rockville Centre man noted in his response, clearly missing life in the city. Most distressing to Long Island boosters, however, was the finding that just 68 percent of those who had moved to the island were happy with their choice, while 81 percent of those who had chosen Westchester and 87 percent of New Jerseyites could say so. In sum, Long Island, which had grown the fastest, was viewed as having the most and worst problems, not a good sign for the future.[243] Indeed, Long Island was about to endure a host of challenges that would make going east to find the American dream an elusive proposition.

Chapter 5

A 118-MILE-LONG METROPOLIS

From a sociologist's viewpoint, Long Island is already much closer
to being a city than it realizes.
—Joe McCarthy, 1964

I n January 1969, four passengers on an unheated, overcrowded and late LIRR train had had enough. Like 150,000 other commuters, the four work colleagues who regularly took the train home to Long Island from the city were not happy with the service provided. It was no secret that the LIRR, which had for a time improved, was as bad as it had ever been in its long history. (One top Nassau County elected official had recently called it a "rolling slum.") The four passengers, aged between twenty and twenty-two years old, decided to make their dissatisfaction known by not handing their tickets to the conductor when asked to do so.[244]

A noble gesture, perhaps, but the conductor expressed little empathy for the protesters' show of activism. He had the passengers removed from the train at the next stop, which happened to be in Brooklyn, where they were arrested on a charge of "theft of service." Unable to produce the $500 each in bail set by a night court judge, the four spent the night in jail. When they were brought to a court in Queens to face the charges, that judge threw the case out, thinking it was a waste of time. In fact, the Queens judge seemed to side with the protesters. "I don't think people should be dumped into a train in which there is no heat and no seats," he remarked.[245]

The woes of the LIRR were a small piece of the major strife facing Long Island in the turbulent 1960s. Buoyed by the construction of the Long Island Expressway (soon nicknamed Distressway), the populations of both Nassau and Suffolk continued to grow, but differently than in past decades. An influx of blue-collar workers and their families was helping make Long Island seem more urban than suburban, and African Americans' fight for civil rights raised awareness of the discrimination they continued to face in education, housing and employment. The Long Island American dream appeared to be fading, as the social, economic and political discord of the times made itself entirely apparent.

THE BRIDGE TO NEW ENGLAND

As the Kennedys prepared to move into the White House, there was a palpable feeling that America was embarking on a new era in its history. Many Long Islanders had a similar sense that the place they had known and perhaps loved had disappeared and that even more change was on the horizon in the name of progress. Indeed, a drive east from the city toward Montauk revealed that most of the farmers and fishermen had moved on and that much of the famous rustic charm of the island had transformed into sprawling new home developments and boxy shopping centers. And while one could understand how there could be an automotive bottleneck leaving or coming back into the city, why were there traffic jams in places like Patchogue, the Moriches and Eastport? Still, more land was for sale, judging by the signs along roads, making one wonder what the island would be like once the ninety-eight-mile Long Island Expressway and sixty-mile Sunrise Highway extension were completed.[246]

Population forecasters certainly believed that more people would be headed east over the next couple of decades. The number of residents in Nassau County would increase from 1,250,000 in 1960 to about 2 million in 1975, experts in such things predicted, while the population of Suffolk (which was more than three times the size of Nassau) would double, from roughly 500,000 to 1 million. The population of each county had already doubled between 1950 and 1960, with a fivefold increase since 1920. Many of these new people would no doubt be children, meaning more schools would be required, which likely meant higher taxes. Taxes in some places, notably Brookhaven, had already jumped over the past year, posing the question of how high they could go should development continue at the same pace. More generally, town and village officials were faced with the challenge of managing growth through zoning and planning in order to retain the character of their communities, especially on the bucolic East End.[247]

Meanwhile, a strike by employees of the LIRR in the summer of 1960 revealed how dependent many Long Islanders were on the train to get to and from work in Manhattan. Each day, 175,000 riders used what was the nation's busiest commuter railroad, forcing a good many of them to improvise.[248] Some came by land, others by sea and still others by air. Extra buses were able to accommodate twenty-five thousand riders, while the others drove themselves or carpooled to the city. As can be imagined, the normally dense commuting traffic became bumper-to-bumper, with some starting out before dawn to beat the rush. Commuters thinking that they knew secret back roads were known to get lost, making quite a story when they finally reached their offices. Flying on a small plane was an option for those who could afford it, while others found seats on chartered boats or yachts (breakfast included on the way in, cocktails on the way out).[249]

Naturally, the individual who probably had the most influence on the transportation networks of both Long Island and New York City weighed in on the chaotic situation. Robert Moses, who had recently relinquished his title as city parks commissioner but held onto that of state park commissioner, offered his thoughts on the subject in October 1960 at a diner in Westbury. Moses believed that a public authority was needed to run the LIRR, as leaving the railroad in private hands posed too great a risk of debilitating strikes like the most recent one. Not surprisingly, however, Moses talked more about cars than trains, thinking that the upcoming New York World's Fair offered an ideal opportunity for road expansion that would benefit Long Island. (Moses had been named head of the fair as well.) This world's fair, to be held in Flushing Meadows on the same site as the 1939–40 fair, would allow completion of "an arterial road system without parallel in any similar metropolitan complex, a system which will serve all of Long Island for all time," he beamed. Moses called on Long Islanders' "undivided support" for such a grand plan, saying that they would be its "chief beneficiaries" during and long after the 1964–65 world's fair.[250]

Moses did not mention another construction project being considered that, if completed, truly would alter not just the transportation network of Long Island but also its physical landscape. There had long been talk of a vehicular bridge across Long Island Sound from the northeastern tip of Long Island to the Rhode Island–Connecticut shore, as such a thing would directly link the island to New England. If built, say, Hamptonites wanting to do some leaf watching in Vermont in the fall would save many hours of driving time, as would Bostonians wishing to attend a party at the Maidstone Club. (Backtracking to the Throgs Neck Bridge or taking a ferry across the Sound could take half a day.) An engineering study completed in 1957 showed that it was possible to create a bridge across the Sound, elevating the idea from mere fantasy. A bridge going across the "Narrows" from Brooklyn to Staten Island was, apparently, becoming a reality (the longest suspension bridge in the world at the time would open in 1964), more reason to more closely study a lengthy span connecting Long Island with New England.[251]

Not just motorists but also government officials, businesspeople, home builders and recreational organizations supported the building of the bridge—or at least seeing if it was indeed possible. More feasibility studies were done in 1961, with a consulting engineering firm taking the lead. The 1957 report, authored by Charles H. Sells (former New York State public works commissioner), envisioned a twenty-five-mile series of causeways and bridges from Orient Point on the island's north fork to Napatree Point, Rhode Island (near the Connecticut state line). Cleverly, Sells had the structure jump across various islands in the Sound to break it up into smaller segments; Plum Island, Great Gull Island and Fishers Island served as ideal "stepping stones." Sells also proposed extending the in-progress Long Island Expressway from Riverhead toward Orient Point, a thirty- to thirty-five-mile addition that likely made Robert Moses very happy. On the other side, the bridge would hook up with US 1 and the Connecticut Turnpike, directly connecting the northeastern United States with Long Island (and points west, notably New York City).[252]

The possibility of there being another link to the mainland made more progressive officials in Suffolk County quite excited. While the county had been much developed, there was much more potential, particularly with regard to the waterfront. Suffolk had 810 miles of shore frontage, but only a small percentage of it was actually being used because it was not particularly accessible. There could be much more boating, sport fishing and other water activities if it was easier to get to the county, pro-development authorities believed, proposing that a bridge to and from New England be built. It was true that Suffolk was the end of the line, with no possibility of extending farther east. The county depended solely on traffic from the west, and it was no secret that going in that direction could be an arduous, time-consuming affair. "Our future may be uncertain because we jut out to sea," said Suffolk county executive H. Lee Dennison. "Much more will be heard soon about the bridge to New England."[253]

The proposed bridge was, to say the least, an ambitious endeavor. First was the sheer length; it would take a motorist about half an hour to get across. Next was the height; the bridge would have to be very tall to allow big ships to go under it. In addition, the waters in the main channel were deep and turbulent, although the completion of the San Francisco–Oakland Bay Bridge proved that such obstacles could be overcome. However, beyond the major engineering challenges to construct such a monumental project and the time involved (ten years to complete, it was believed), there was the cost, which was estimated to be $300 million ($3 billion today).[254]

Even Robert Moses couldn't find that kind of money in the state's budget, suggesting that the federal government would have to pick up most of the tab. Rather conveniently, the federal interstate highway system was still being constructed, so if the bridge could be part of that, Uncle Sam would pay 90 percent of the cost. New York State and either Rhode Island or Connecticut would share the remaining 10 percent, a much more manageable number for Suffolk County officials to sell to the state legislature. Having the federal government pay for most of the cost would also allow the structure not to be a toll bridge, something that both politicians and voters despised in general. It would take many years for a state to recover the expense of building a bridge across Long Island Sound by motorists dropping spare change into a bucket.[255]

THIS SERIOUS AMERICAN DILEMMA

While civil engineers pondered whether such a structure could be built without bankrupting a state or the country, more pressing matters surfaced in the 1960s for Long Island. New Jersey had stood up to William Levitt and his fellow racists and set an example for other states to follow. The vast majority of builders and real estate developers in New York State favored a similar ban on discrimination in private housing, saying as much in a public hearing in Albany in January 1960. Not only was it unfair, but it was also bad business, they made clear at the hearing organized by Senator George Metcalf, as excluding a market as sizable as people of color just didn't make economic sense. As well, racial bias encouraged the flourishing of slums, the group agreed, and that hurt real estate values in nearby areas. Finally, with urban renewal and redevelopment, it was difficult for African Americans to find anywhere to live, especially if most suburban developments wanted nothing to do with them (even if they could afford it). More moderately priced rentals and older homes for sale were needed, although an antibias bill such as the one the senator had cosponsored would go a long way toward making it possible for African Americans with a steady income to get their piece of the American dream.[256]

Just not having one's home burned down by racists was a concern for Long Island African Americans, however. Like the home of Clarence Wilson, which was repeatedly set on fire while it was being built in an all-White neighborhood in 1953, that of Eloise Kirkland met the same fate seven years later in all-White section of Freeport. The fire was set the very night she and her family moved in (from an unheated shack near the LIRR tracks), with bits of charred paper found at the scene. The Kirklands continued to move in with their possessions, but a few days later, the house was gutted by flames. Freeport fire chief Ryder found a penny that had been inserted into the fuse box, which short-circuited wires and apparently caused the blaze, while Freeport mayor William Glacken conceded he had received about a dozen calls from neighbors allegedly concerned about whether the house was "suitable for habitation."[257]

Things went better for David Pinckney when he and his family moved from Hempstead to Kensington, an "exclusive" section of Great Neck. Pinckney, an African American physician, and his family were what the *Atlanta Daily World* called the "first of their race" to live in that area. Pinckney was the highest bidder on the English Tudor house that was valued at $50,000 and was sold by the McCowans, who were moving to Virginia. The McCowans received a number of anonymous phone calls from people upset about their selling the house to a Black family, but that appeared to be the only negative response to news of the sale. Helping things in that regard was the formation of an organization calling itself the Human Rights Committee of Great Neck, whose purpose was to fight discrimination in local home sales. "Panic selling" when a family of color moved into a White neighborhood was known to take place, and Great Neckers did not want that to happen in their beautiful town.[258]

The Pinckneys' move into a tony part of already tony Great Neck made good copy for the nation's African American newspapers. "Soul-searching swank Long Island community drops anti-bias attitudes," read a headline for the *Chicago Daily Defender*, a breath of fresh air against the backdrop of redlining and worse for Black homeowners. The Human Rights Committee of Great Neck was formed in part because of local children's beliefs about African Americans. "They assumed all Negroes were servants," explained Mary Calderone, chair of the committee, with parents so shocked they felt their group had to make it more possible for children to have African Americans as neighbors. The Pinckneys were first, but more Black families were on the way; another home had been rented to a writer and his family while two more sales—one to a lawyer and the other to a business executive—were pending. Again, anonymous people called sellers who cared more about a buyer's financial resources than the color of his and his family's skin, but they were typically not threatening enough to limit a sale to a White buyer or take the house off the market.[259]

The Human Rights Committee of Great Neck had an interesting beginning. Black teachers had been hired by the town's excellent public school system but were refused housing in the community. Then, on seeing an African American teacher, one child asked his mother whose maid she was, prompting that mother to bring up the issue at the next PTA meeting. (It was true: most of the two thousand Blacks who lived in Great Neck worked as domestics for the well-to-do but lived in the other, segregated part of town.) Soon, the organization was founded and by July 1961 had 350 dues-paying members. Even more impressive, more than thirty homeowners had agreed to list their homes for sale without prejudice, going against the grain of most other fashionable towns in northern Nassau.[260]

Not everybody had fifty grand to buy a house, however, regardless of their skin color, meaning different solutions had to be found if Long Island communities were eventually going to be integrated. Recognizing the problem, the Long Island CORE (Congress of Racial Equality) started its own clearinghouse of residential listings in predominantly White neighborhoods where people of color were encouraged to seek to buy a home. Thirty such houses were listed within a few days, but just a few people applied for them, meaning there were more sellers than buyers. CORE then put an ad in the *New York Times* listing the houses for sale, hoping that would stir interest, and the organization planned to further spread the message by reaching out to African American groups. Regardless of such a list, many Blacks remained justifiably fearful of moving into a White area of Long Island, knowing full well the possible repercussions.[261]

While Blacks were invited to try to be homeowners in certain White neighborhoods at their own risk, urban renewal programs in four towns were displacing thousands of African American residents. "Clearance" and "reconstruction" operations were scheduled to evict about six hundred Black families from their homes in Long Beach, Glen Cove, Rockville Centre and Huntington Station, with few options for where they could relocate. The New York State NAACP protested the programs, with picket lines formed in Rockville Centre and Long Beach on a cold winter day in December 1961. Despite CORE's listings, African Americans were not welcome in most White areas of Long Island, forcing families to leave their communities for parts unknown. New York State had paid for half of the urban renewal programs, making it complicit in what Jack Wood of the NAACP termed "Long Island prejudice."[262]

It had already been established that the real estate business was rife with discriminatory practices, with more evidence of that surfacing in 1962. In a clever test, CORE had teams of African American couples and White couples attempt to buy houses in forty different all-White neighborhoods. The Black couples went first, but in all cases but one, realtors gave reasons other than skin color for why the sale couldn't take place. Then the White couples followed, and in every case, the realtors were happy to make a deal. No fewer than 150 transactions were attempted by each couple, enough data to suggest that realtors were reinforcing segregation in many Long Island communities.[263]

Both CORE and the NAACP were certainly busy on Long Island in the early 1960s, doing what they could to fight racial discrimination on a number of fronts. In 1962, the NAACP filed two civil suits charging school segregation in Amityville and Manhasset. (A case against a Hempstead district had already been filed.) In 1954, the Supreme Court had unanimously ruled that racial segregation in public schools was unconstitutional (even if "separate but equal"), but the NAACP argued that two school districts were maintaining the practice. The districts appeared to be sorting by skin color in determining which schools the thirty-six students (twenty-two in Amityville and fourteen in Manhasset) should attend, a clear violation of federal law. The NAACP had tried to persuade the districts to voluntarily stop the practice, but the discussions failed, hence the legal action.[264]

A couple of weeks later, a Westbury school district became the fourth on Long Island to be sued by the NAACP over alleged segregation. It appeared that various communities in Nassau County were resisting racial integration of schools, specifically by building new schools in locations that would ensure segregated enrollment or by more blatant measures.[265] In Westbury, for example, White students in school buses were actually passing a Black school (New Cassel) on the way to their own (Park). The Westbury school superintendent claimed that his establishment of attendance zones was based on "convenience and economy," but that would be for a judge to decide.[266] The *Baltimore Afro-American* labeled this kind of discrimination

"Yankee brand segregation," a more subtle but equally immoral version of racism than that taking place at the same time in the Deep South.[267]

Not subtle was what was reported to be "Long Island's first racial sit-in" to protest "de facto" school segregation in Malverne. The event took place in an office at Malverne Junior High School while the local school board was holding a meeting in the auditorium. Three adults (two Black, one White) were the leaders of the protest, with thirty-one others (twenty Black, eleven White) picketing with signs nearby. The three leaders (all members of the Long Island CORE) had fasted for twenty-four hours before occupying the administrative office and ended the vigil at eighty thirty that evening when they issued a statement. "Few people, Negro or white, can claim unawareness of this serious American dilemma, of which the situation in Malverne School District 12 is only one facet," their statement read.[268] Malverne was soon added to the NAACP's legal action list, as was Glen Cove.[269]

THE SUB-THEME OF RACE

The sit-in and handful of NAACP lawsuits appeared to work. In September 1962, it was announced that about eighty African American students in the Hempstead district would be allowed to transfer from their segregated and overcrowded schools to predominantly White ones. This was reported to be the first attempt on Long Island to end de facto segregation and, ultimately, integrate schools. The NAACP called the move a step in the right direction but not a long enough step. The organization made a good point; the Hempstead school district had about 3,400 elementary pupils, and 57 percent of them were Black, making the transfer a proverbial drop in the ocean. The NAACP was in favor of the "Princeton plan," which provided centralized schools for each grade that were attended by all children, regardless of race, in the district.[270]

Progress against discrimination was being made in other ways, due largely to efforts by the NAACP and CORE. Larger companies on Long Island had been resistant to hiring African Americans as employees, something CORE made note of. After considerable discussion, Hicksville-based Franklin National Bank, one of the biggest banks on the island, agreed to hire a greater number of Black and Puerto Rican employees, something that CORE considered "a major breakthrough." The bank's management agreed to "initiate a more vigorous program of minority recruitment," according to a company statement, a good thing given that just 15 of the bank's 1,200 employees were African American.[271]

The year 1963 appeared to be somewhat of a tipping point in race relations, as African Americans made some gains in equal rights in education, work and even high society. For the first time in its sixty-eight-year history, the East Hampton Ladies Village Improvement Society admitted a Black member that year. The newest member of the elite club was Mrs. Robert Hamilton, a former schoolteacher who also belonged to the East Hampton Guild Hall and the South Park Craftsman's Guild. Hamilton received thirty ayes and eighteen nays when the vote for her membership was taken by the club, whose mission was to raise money to make East Hampton even more beautiful.[272]

While some positive things were happening to lessen the virulent racism in Nassau County, local activists continued to apply pressure to the powers that be. CORE and the NAACP were working together in 1964 to register as many Black voters as possible to shape legislation. (Fifteen thousand African Americans in the county were eligible to vote.) The voter drive was focused on ending segregated education in Glen Cove, a town that had yet to move toward limited integration as in Hempstead. Glen Cove had a particularly ugly history in its treatment of both African Americans and Puerto Ricans. Alleged urban renewal programs had, over the past five years, forced nearly one hundred families of color out of what was labeled a ghetto, yet no actual "renewal" had taken place. With not a single brick laid, the programs were clearly designed to simply remove the families from the generally White and affluent town, with no relocation efforts provided.[273]

Racism had existed on Long Island well before the heyday of the KKK in the 1920s, of course, but "now the sub-theme of race persists throughout the cacophony of problems created by the burgeoning urban complex," George Barner wrote for the *Amsterdam News* in 1965. As the population of Blacks on Long Island grew during and after World War II, in large part because of defense jobs, the issue of race increasingly intersected with inequalities embedded in housing, employment, education, politics and other key dimensions of society. By the mid-1960s, with the civil rights movement continually gaining traction, it was impossible to ignore the reality of discrimination and efforts to end it, particularly in Nassau County. Given the battles taking place on many fronts, one might have thought that African Americans represented a sizable portion of the county, but that would be incorrect. Blacks comprised just about 45,000 (3.2 percent) of the county's total population of 1.3 million people, according to a study by the Nassau County Planning Commission, although their numbers continued to increase.[274]

Statistics from 1960 also revealed the bad hand Long Island African Americans were dealt, especially with regard to work. Blacks were paid less (even if they had the same education level as a White colleague), given fewer opportunities to advance and had fewer job opportunities (even if they had similar skills as a White candidate). Married African American women were more likely to work than White women because of this wage disparity based on skin color. (Of the non-White labor force, 42 percent were employed as domestic household workers, rather incredibly, while the number was between 1 percent and 2 percent for Whites.) The household income of a Black family on Long Island was about $3,000 less than that of a White family, even though more members of the former were likely to be employed. Finally, African Americans were twice as likely as Whites of a similar age to be unemployed, census data showed, not too surprising given prevailing racial attitudes on the island in the 1960s. "In Nassau County, which prides itself on being a liberal, progressive community, the non-white is greatly disadvantaged by his skin color," a 1965 Hofstra University study concluded.[275]

If the odds were distinctly stacked against Blacks in the workplace, the game was positively fixed in terms of housing. Although just a small part of Long Island's total population, African Americans were routinely siloed in designated neighborhoods or effectively forced to relocate to another part of the state or country. Housing was the key to broader racial discrimination, the Hofstra study found. "Residential segregation provides a basic structure and rationale, and indeed a stimulus, for many other forms of segregation," wrote Stefan Leader, a coauthor of the study, finding that Blacks and Whites not living near each other had a ripple effect throughout society. "The result more often than not is segregation in schools, recreation, shopping, theaters, hospitals and many other public accommodations." Landlords of African American tenants intentionally allowed their rented houses or apartments to deteriorate, Hofstra's research showed, a means to both save money and create the "slums" or "ghettos" that could eventually qualify for urban renewal development.[276]

With holes in the walls, broken tile floors, leaking plumbing, rickety stairways and menagerie of rats and roaches in their building, tenants of the Wilkow Apartments in Hempstead had had enough. In 1965, they held Long Island's first rent strike, first refusing to pay their landlord the five-dollar monthly increase he demanded. CORE then joined the action, and the full rent strike began, which certainly got the attention of the landlord (a rabbi, no less). After negotiations, an agreement was reached in which the landlord agreed to repair each apartment and the building, build a playground and replace appliances. Leading the effort for CORE was Geraldine Johnson, a former resident of Montgomery, Alabama, who had taken part in the historic 1956 bus boycott held there. Johnson had recently met with Martin Luther King Jr. when the reverend came to Hempstead for a rally and a CORE-sponsored tour of the depressed area.[277]

Issues of class within the African American community surfaced in New Cassel, which was almost 40 percent Black. More than half of the African Americans in that town owned their homes and had a median household income of $16,000, which was 60 percent higher than that of Blacks nationwide. Many of these middle-class residents had fled Harlem, the South Bronx and Bedford-Stuyvesant to escape the economic and social problems of those areas of New York City. More lower-class African Americans were taking up residence in New Cassel in the mid-sixties, however, a result of the widespread displacement of Blacks from other Long Island communities. The more prosperous New Casselites were not happy to see the influx of domestics and welfare recipients moving in, an interesting case of class dynamics at work within the broader context of race.[278]

Long City

The escalating racial tensions on Long Island in the mid-1960s were in part a function of the island's phenomenal growth. The year 1964 was the 350th anniversary of its first appearance on a map as an island, cause for journalist, author and Long Islander Joe McCarthy to reflect on how it had evolved, particularly in recent decades. "Once consecrated to potato farms and the estates of the rich, Long Island is fast turning into a 118-mile-long metropolis," his piece for the *New York Times Magazine* began. McCarthy believed that the place had always had its own distinct identity. The island's amazing geographic diversity—sand dunes on the outer beaches, the green and hilly North Shore, pine barrens in the middle, flat farmlands in Suffolk and an almost Old South feeling on the remaining grand estates—was a microcosm of America. Add a whaling port, the chic Hampton resorts, dozens of private and public golf courses, some of the best sport fishing to be found anywhere and the wonder that was Jones Beach, and one could see why so many people visited Long Island or decided to call it home.[279]

The growth of Long Island was indeed rather startling. While the East End was still quite rural and agricultural (a couple of one-room schoolhouses could still be found), other areas had exploded over the past decade, fueled in large part by the baby boom. In 1954, for example, there was one school with 250 pupils in Commack, but ten years later, there were 12,000 students in eighteen schools. Other towns in Suffolk, such as Smithtown, could tell a similar story, but it was Nassau County where even bigger changes could be seen. Farmland and the carefully tended gardens of private estates were now square or rectangular lawns, many of them with swing sets and slides. Basketball had become more popular than baseball because it took up a smaller space to play, and recently, the seven-year locusts had decided not to make their annual appearance as their host trees and grasslands had been turned into housing. Long Island's pre-1950 almost feudal economy, consisting of estate employees, farmers, fishermen and tradesmen, had transformed into a commuting, manufacturing and retail workforce, a kind of compressed, mini–Industrial Revolution that took about fifteen years.[280]

Roads, of course, had much to do with the growth of Long Island. Before 1950, one wanting to use a public road to get anywhere relatively quickly had an easy choice: Merrick Road/Montauk Highway on the South Shore or Jericho Turnpike on the North Shore. Robert Moses had done much to change that, primarily to make the outer beaches and newly built parks accessible from Manhattan and the mainland. The creation of a network of parkways, bridges and tunnels served as the means to do that, something that was ideally aligned with Detroit's mass production of the automobile. Many children who had visited Long Island in the 1930s with their families became homebuyers in the late 1940s and 1950s, perhaps not suspecting how much time the breadwinner would spend commuting to and from the city.[281]

Against logic, no addition or expansion of roads on Long Island appeared to be sufficient to handle the amount of traffic. The Long Island Expressway was not complete in 1964, yet already motorists were declaring it inadequate. (Its label as the "longest parking lot in the world" had also already been established.) Some were saying an upper deck needed to be added to the expressway in Queens to accommodate some of the more than one hundred thousand vehicles a day that currently used the road. Traffic in the air was almost as congested. More than three thousand passenger planes a day went in and out of Kennedy, La Guardia and Islip's MacArthur Airports, with a couple dozen of them frequently in a holding pattern over Long Island.

For whatever reason, the airspace over Deer Park seemed to be the favorite among pilots waiting to land.[282]

More than anything else, however, it was the redistribution of land after World War I that redefined Long Island. Rising land values and taxes, plus the increasing difficulty of getting good help those days as the managerial class emerged, meant the end of most of the grand estates. Gatsby-like mansions and their grounds were either turned into lots or repurposed as colleges and schools or conservation preserves. Still, however, Suffolk County farmers were producing plenty of potatoes, breeders were raising loads of ducks (two-thirds of the nation's total) and growers were cultivating heaps of plants, flowers, fruits and vegetables.[283]

Most tellingly for McCarthy, who had unsurpassed insights about Long Island culture, it was the urbanization of the island over the past decade and a half that was remarkable. A good number of the members of the one-class white-collar society of Levittown and its sibling developments of mid-century had, by the mid-'60s, moved on to better jobs and bigger houses. Those "original settlers," as McCarthy called them, were being replaced by "a new influx of blue-collar industrial and mechanical workers fresh from Brooklyn, the Bronx, and Queens who bring to the suburbs a city

A roadside attraction circa 1972 that clearly conveyed one of the things for which Long Island was famous. *Margolies, John, photographer. "Long Island duck, Long Island, New York."*

dweller's attitude, tastes and prejudices." The numbers bore out McCarthy's observation: nearly half of Levittown's residents were blue-collar families. There were, in short, two distinct subclasses within the White middle class, a major shift in Long Island's social, economic and political orientation.[284]

The change in demographics had significant implications for employment. With more blue-collar workers moving to Long Island from the city, more local jobs were needed, as these were not the white-collar managers commuting to a Manhattan office. Industry had to be expanded, in other words, especially given the recent decline of defense jobs. Elected officials were trying to lure more plants and factories to Long Island to avoid high rates of unemployment (and to support the high tax rate). Suffolk County was in worse shape than Nassau in this respect, as 40 percent of wage earners in the latter did commute to well-paid jobs in the city.[285]

There were other signs that Long Island was becoming more urbanized, at least in a cultural sense. Drug use and addiction were on the rise, for example, surprising many who believed that such practices magically stopped moving east at the Queens border. In April 1965, there was a major arrest of suspected drug addicts and pushers on Long Island, an action that happened to be timed with a seminar at Hofstra University led by Robert W. Baird, director of the Harlem Narcotics Rehabilitation Center (aka the Haven). Baird told the audience of four hundred attendees that the number of addicts said to be on the island was very underreported, having had experience with people with that problem from Atlantic Beach, Babylon, Cedarhurst, Great Neck, Mineola, Wantagh, Bay Shore and other communities. Baird, who was a practicing physician, was especially upset about the over-the-counter sale of cough medicine that included codeine as an ingredient, finding it to be a common source of addiction among young people.[286]

Of course, Long Island was urbanized every weekend from Memorial Day to Labor Day as tens of thousands of city folk headed to the East End. While the wealthy might sail or helicopter to their summer homes in the Hamptons (complete with privet hedges), the hoi polloi took the LIRR or endured the bumper-to-bumper traffic to reach an untidy house filled with as many as a dozen other shares. (Staying in one of the many motels on NY 27—"Free TV and air-conditioning!"—was another option, although a surprising number of "beatniks" slept on the beach.) Some weekenders boated, fished, surfed or played golf or tennis, but most went to party and make new friends and lovers. For now, the East End, with its cloud-gray shingled houses and windmills, remained as picturesque as anywhere, but one had to wonder if some entrepreneur would eventually Levittownize it.[287]

A simulated moon landing at Grumman Aviation in 1969 not long before the real thing. *Gotfryd, Bernard, photographer. "Simulated moon landing at Grumman Aviation Long Island, New York."*

A lunar vehicle at Grumman Aviation in 1969 in preparation for the historic *Apollo 11* flight. *Gotfryd, Bernard, photographer. "Lunar vehicle at Grumman's, L.I., Apollo 11."*

Heresy, perhaps, but the impetus to expand Long Island's economy to meet the needs of a larger population was reason to consider additional links to the mainland. A bridge from Orient Point (or perhaps Riverhead, some were now thinking) across the Sound to Connecticut or Rhode Island was one possibility, but planners and business leaders were pondering other options. "Should new routes serve planes (another airport or two), trains (a high-speed railroad) or automobiles (another tunnel)?" they asked themselves, a definitive answer unclear. The desire for more routes to encourage more industry was understandable but a bit odd given the fact that the local economy was doing just fine. Nationally, the postwar economic engine was running out of steam, while employment, personal income and business and consumer spending had all reached new highs in 1966, according to the Franklin National Bank. Farmers in Suffolk County had raised crops worth more than $70 million, more than any other county in the state.[288]

Even the defense business on Long Island, which had shown clear signs of lagging in the early '60s, was robust in the latter part of the decade (in large part because the Vietnam War was escalating). Grumman had, for the first time, passed $1 billion in sales, not surprising given that the corporation produced eight types of warplanes, NASA's "moonship," hydrofoil boats and crop-dusting (and -destroying) planes. Republic Aviation had declined after it was bought out by Fairchild Hiller but was successfully diversifying and again profitable. All good news, but where more industry should go was a conundrum. Just a few hundred acres of development land was left in Nassau County (recalling the western frontier of the United States closing in 1890), and planners considered Suffolk to be a dead end whose economic value was largely limited to agriculture and tourism.[289]

The Great Wall of China

A few years after his astute 1964 piece in the *New York Times Magazine*, Joe McCarthy weighed in again on the state of Long Island in the same publication. This time, his focus was the Long Island Expressway (LIE), mostly complete but hardly the solution to the island's legendary transportation problems. Traffic often stretched all the way from the Queens Midtown Tunnel well into Suffolk County in both directions, a stream of colorful lights that could be seen from space. Where so many people were going or coming from was unclear, but there was no doubt that the new main commuting and commercial trucking artery between New York City and Long Island's suburbs was a mess. The (ironically named) expressway—which had taken thirteen years to build and, in 1967, still had thirty miles of construction remaining to reach its goal of Riverhead—was already one of the most congested roads in the country. Traffic on it was getting worse rather than better as it lengthened, even during non-rush hours. A stalled or broken-down car or a crash shutting down a lane or two was a nightmare for motorists that recalled the famous "Blue Monday" automobile scrum in Boston on December 30, 1963, which lasted close to twelve hours.[290]

As always with roads connecting New York City with Long Island, Queens was the major problem. There were simply too many cars for the six-lane expressway (three in each direction), with critics (including New York City traffic commissioner Henry Barnes) thinking it had to be at least eight to handle the volume in that borough. Adding lanes would be almost like starting from scratch, however, and thus not going to happen given the construction cost of $2 million per mile. Public Works engineers defended the decision for six lanes, however, thinking that the traffic jams on the LIE were mild compared to those that took place in Los Angeles, which had no equivalent to the LIRR to ease the commuter load.[291]

Although that view was cold comfort to a regular user of the LIE, it couldn't be denied that the road had led to higher employment in the outer suburbs. Jobs in defense plants, schools, shopping centers and construction had increased as the expressway reached further east, creating a significant reverse commute from the city. And unlike the Northern and Southern State Parkways, the LIE allowed commercial vehicles, a good many of them carrying building materials for use by land developers, particularly in Suffolk (the fastest-growing county in the state and possibly the country). Nassau was a much different story, as the road crossed through older, mostly upscale residential communities such as Lake Success, Manhasset, Roslyn and Westbury. "It cuts through here like the Great Wall of China!" a Roslynite barked, not able to hear his television if the windows of his house were open and finding a perpetual film of oil on the windows. A Syosset resident who used the LIE to commute to the city had a novel solution to the problematic road. "The only thing to do about the Long Island Expressway is to close Long Island," he quipped.[292]

If Suffolk county executive H. Lee Dennison had his way, however, Long Island would be further opened up rather than closed. Dennison, who had argued for some time that a bridge across the Sound should be anchored in Riverhead rather than Orient Point, now believed that there should be not one, not two but three such bridges. One of them, he suggested in 1968, should serve a mid-Sound jetport located on a to-be-built artificial island. It's unclear what Dennison had ingested when he presented his vision, but yachtsmen, conservationists and other anti-bridgers were not happy to hear it. Currently, two more realistic proposals were being floated. The first was a 6.5-mile bridge from Bayville in eastern Nassau to Rye on the Westchester shore (estimated cost $160 million), and the second a 14.6-mile span from Port Jefferson to Bridgeport, Connecticut ($225 million). Robert Moses (now chairman of the Triborough Bridge Authority) endorsed the former plan, criticizing the yacht racers' idea to build a tunnel under rather than a bridge over the Sound so the span wouldn't interfere with their oversized boats.[293]

While key players went back and forth over how to bring more drivers (and their money) to Long Island from New England, going largely ignored were serious problems with a form of transportation that had been around for well over a century. "To be dependent on the Long Island Rail Road is to need no other aggravation," Martin Arnold of the *New York Times* wrote in 1968 after the latest incident, a total shutdown for two days due to a trainmen's strike that affected some ninety thousand commuters (on Thanksgiving, ironically). Relying on the LIRR to get

A 1968 photo of the Manhasset Bridge, over which the much-maligned LIRR passed. *Historic American Engineering Record, creator; Sharpe, David, photographer. "Long Island Railroad, Manhasset Bridge, Manhasset Shore Road Vicinity, Flower Hill, Nassau County, NY."*

to and from work was a distinct hazard, although many commuters had simply gotten used to the suffering (and the surly conductors) that came with it.[294] One thousand people showed up at the January 1969 hearing of the Joint Legislative Committee on Mass Transportation in Garden City to let LIRR management know how they felt about the stifling hot, freezing cold, dangerously crowded, sometimes unlighted cars and having to explain to bosses yet again why they were late to work. Getting trapped in a smoky tunnel was a truly frightening and potentially dangerous situation that passengers on one train had recently experienced.[295]

The 1969 kerfuffle over the four passengers who wouldn't pay their fare until service was improved was an indication of how bad the LIRR had become. "For the past few months, the Long Island Rail Road has been declining from the status of a fourth-rate public conveyance to that of a first-class public nuisance," an editor for the *New York Times* wrote six months after the protesters were arrested for their action. Cancellations and taking a couple of cars off trains for some reason were daily occurrences, with many passengers routinely having to stand for an hour in a narrow aisle. The luckier passengers had the privilege of sitting in dirty seats with poking springs while looking out dirty windows, some of them literally taped together. Often unheated in the winter months, the cars were as frequently not air-conditioned in the summer, making a typical ride on the LIRR a dreaded and dreadful experience.[296]

Adding insult to injury was the fact that commuter fares were hardly cheap—typically more than $40 a month ($320 today)—perhaps because the LIRR needed lots of cash to pay victims' families when there was a collision. (One had just taken place near Penn Station.) Ninety-four new cars had been ordered; however, none of them worked, and the union wouldn't have its members repair them until a deal could be reached, not at all a good situation. (Of the LIRR's 7,000 employees, 6,500 worked in one or more of seventeen different labor unions.)[297] The LIRR had commissioned study after study to find solutions to its many problems, yet things seemed to be getting worse rather than better. Inept management appeared to be the real problem, but apparently, the authors of the studies did not recommend replacing the people who had commissioned them.[298] In July 1969, however, Governor Rockefeller was seriously considering asking the MTA's board to fire the railroad's president, Frank Aikman Jr. (in part because the LIRR's many woes had become a political liability).[299] A few days later, Aikman decided to take early retirement.[300]

With Aikman out, Rockefeller (who would soon be running for reelection) promised that the LIRR would offer the best railroad service in America in just two months, a prediction that proved to be overambitious. In fact, just a couple of weeks after the governor's pledge, twenty-six rush-hour trains were canceled on a single day, an all-time high. A new system was in place, a spokesperson for the LIRR explained, but representatives of a couple of the six commuter groups that had recently been formed were skeptical. (Even the head of the railroad's unionized engineers said that Rockefeller's assurance was "sheer nonsense.") Simply lowering expectations seemed to be a wiser choice than expecting great service from the railroad; a train just fifteen minutes late was judged by some to be early. There was no chance that the LIRR would be the best railroad in America, but it was entirely safe to say that it would be the only one on Long Island.[301]

As the amazing summer of 1969 (both Woodstock and the first landing on the moon had taken place) wound down, a relatively minor but telling event took place on Long Island. The lifeguards at the island's state parks threatened to go on strike if the beaches were closed after Labor Day weekend, as the commission had said it was going to do for budget reasons. The season had always run until October 1, and the lifeguards made it clear that they would walk off their towers before Labor Day should that be the plan. (California lifeguards may have been mellow, but their Long Island cousins were a feisty bunch; the latter had struck a couple of years previously to get a twenty-five-cent-an-hour wage increase.) The good news that the commission had found an extra $200,000 to keep the beaches open through October averted the walkout, but the chaos that defined the 1960s on Long Island was not at all over.[302]

Chapter 6

THE DREAM DEFERRED

It [Long Island] *can be one of the worst areas in the world* [but] *there is
enough of it left to make it one of the most beautiful and wonderful.*
—*H. Lee Dennison, Suffolk county executive, 1971*

In 1979, shades of Long Island's more intriguing past could be found
on both its North and South Shores. Drug smugglers were finding the
island's scenic coves, inlets and beaches very amenable to unloading
their illegal, mind-altering substances from boats. Law enforcement
agencies and the Coast Guard were doing what they could to stop this
importing of highly profitable goods but intercepting only 10 to 20 percent
of the traffic into the island. New York City was the ultimate destination
for the stuff, making Long Island's lengthy, largely unpatrolled shoreline
an ideal drop-off point. The smuggling was eerily similar to the rum-
running activity that took place on Long Island during Prohibition in the
1920s and early 1930s, although now it was tons of marijuana, cocaine
and quaaludes that were coming ashore rather than cases of rum, scotch
and whiskey.[303]

That Long Island had become a favored port of call for drug smugglers
was just one of many problems confronted on the island in the wild and
woolly 1970s. Now, half a century after land speculators and realtors
first spotted the enormous opportunity to move cramped New Yorkers
eastward, Long Island was said to have come of age, not an entirely good

thing. While commuting culture still played a major role in everyday life, the island had become less dependent on the city to the west. The postwar economic engine had by now shut down, however, and inflation plus high property taxes were making it difficult for the middle class to make ends meet. Other problems, such as persistent race discrimination in housing, an increasingly polluted environment and endless traffic jams despite all the highways that had been built with much fanfare, were reasons why some Long Islanders were calling moving trucks. The American dream was not only expensive, many were thinking to themselves, but was it now even possible?

The Outer City

Writing for *Newsday* in 1970, Philip L. Greene told his story of moving from New York City to Long Island in pursuit of the wide-open spaces, remaining farmland and the "good life." Greene described the suburbs as "Out Here," a perspective that reflected his roots in the inner city. The classic activities of suburban life—owning a house, driving a car, commuting to the city and being surrounded by nature—were for him an alien and "faintly criminal" experience, as if he had invaded a foreign territory belonging to "them." As a first-generation Jewish American raised in Brooklyn, Greene grew up with a sense of otherness, a feeling that he couldn't help transferring to his odyssey to the suburbs. But this was for Greene a necessary step for him to feel truly American, a journey that would allow him to be released from his marginalized urban past.[304]

Greene's take on Long Island circa 1970 was a valuable one, if only because he viewed the place with fresh eyes. One of his early observations after migrating east was how the public street life of the city shifted to a private backyard life of the suburbs. Moving from the front porch to a patio changed the dynamic one had with one's neighbors and the larger community, with fences and shrubs adding to the feeling of insularity. Greene jumped into the standard lifestyle quickly, however, painting his house, restoring the lawn and chatting with the neighbors over the fence. Going to PTA meetings, playing cards with new friends and getting on a first-name basis with the mailman and garbageman were part of the routine. "City friends came, and we chided them about high rents and clogged subways and dirty and dangerous streets," Greene recalled, his conversion apparently complete.[305]

A Long Island farm circa 1970 that had survived development, at least for the moment. *Gotfryd, Bernard, photographer. "Farm on LI."*

Naturally, things were not perfect despite the former urbanite and his family seemingly achieving their American dream. Taxes were high and getting higher, and inflation was making everything more expensive. (The inflation rate in the United States in 1970 was 6 percent.) The nation's political and social problems of the times—the Vietnam War, student protests, racial unrest, pollution—were bummers, of course, but it was suburbanites' obsession with materialism that was most disconcerting. "In the suburbs you live through your materiality, which is the visible symbol of your life," Greene wrote; he thought people's love of things was the greatest failure of his adopted community. Even more than desiring new things, Long Islanders were terrified of losing what they already had, something Greene had never encountered in the city. "People are friendly but mistrustful," he concluded, still navigating his way through this strange new land.[306]

Six months later, Jack Rosenthal of the *New York Times* offered his thoughts on what he called the "outer city." (The newspaper had sent Rosenthal and four other reporters across the United States to "explore the growth, complexities and attitudes of suburban America.") For Rosenthal, Long Island and its suburban cousins represented "a new form of urban settlement…no longer mere orbital satellites" of their original host cities.

By any measure, the suburbs were now cities in their own right, he believed, this despite having no center. Over the past two decades, much of the nation's White middle class had abandoned cities for the suburbs, with some thinking that in another twenty years, urban America would consist almost completely of poor people of color.[307]

It was not a secret that the development of the suburbs was first and foremost about land, specifically how to make money by buying and selling it. With its 775 municipalities, New York City had the largest and most valuable suburban area in the world, all of it within one hundred miles of Times Square. Battles for control over the land were a common feature in most of those municipalities, the *Times* reporters had found, especially in the New York suburbs because of their generally high value. Oddly, perhaps, much of this control had to do with keeping new people out of communities, with zoning regulations the primary means of doing that. Variances and special exceptions could be made, such as the ones being offered in 1971 by the town of Smithtown, but they would likely cost a pretty penny. Money under the table was sometimes passed to the powers that be to develop or not develop a particular property, with deals often not in the interests of low- or middle-income residents but rather to get rich people richer. *Newsday*, which had reached a circulation of 458,000, investigated such shady dealings, leading to a few greedy local officials ending up in jail.[308]

Low- or middle-income people thinking about buying the kind of one-family house that Long Island was famous for were in for a rude surprise when learning how much such a thing would now cost. Land, labor and materials had all risen significantly in recent years, putting a starter home out of reach for many young couples. "Whatever happened to the American dream of the honeymoon cottage?" asked developer Murray Barbash, with newlyweds either finding the cost too high or what they would get not up to their expectations. Rent, too, had gone up, so much so that some couples were moving in with their parents to try to save money for a future purchase. Income had not kept up with costs because of inflation and the scarcity of land to develop on the island. It was easy to look back on the postwar years with a sense of wistfulness, wishing one had bought a nice $10,000–$12,000 home when all one needed was $5,000 in annual income. Such a house now cost $32,000, way too much for the junior businessman or other worker with similar pay.[309]

There was no doubt that the economy of Long Island and the nation as a whole was not a healthy one for the middle class. There was "a money squeeze," Frank Corrigan of *Newsday* wrote, and "LIers are feeling the pinch." People whose incomes were higher than ever often felt more financially insecure than ever, a paradox that stemmed from the rate of inflation and tax schedules. Nixon administration wage and price controls were in effect but, because of loopholes, seemed to have little impact on the actual cost of living, a frustrating situation for the average breadwinner. "Many of us here on the Island thought we had attained the Great American Dream of a house in the suburbs, two cars, a great place to raise the kids," Phylis Stetson of Levittown wrote in a letter to *Newsday*, finding it difficult to balance her household's budget despite her husband having two jobs. Some Long Islanders unable to make ends meet were having to sell their houses and move someplace cheaper to live, their dream having become a nightmare.[310]

Levittown was celebrating its twenty-fifth anniversary in 1972, an occasion to reflect on how it and its residents had evolved since 1947. The average price of a house in the mammoth community was now $29,500, quite a bit more than their original price of $6,990 or $7,990. It was not unusual for children of the original residents to now, as adults, have homes in Levittown, even if they hadn't been happy to move there with their families from the city. (Getting lost because all the streets looked the same was a common complaint.) Seeing old friends from childhood days while shopping at Roosevelt Field was a pleasant experience that brought back happy memories, and seeing how big the five hundred thousand trees Levitt & Sons had planted had become was also enjoyable. There was more crime now, and the generation gap could make family life more challenging, but overall, Levittown retained much of its initial appeal. As evidence of that, the population of Levittown was documented at 65,440 in the 1970 census, making it the largest unincorporated community in the United States.[311]

While a small percentage of Levittown's current residents were African American, race-based discrimination remained woven into Long Island's real estate market. Civil rights activism and the passage of laws had chipped away at some of the blatant efforts to keep Blacks out of predominantly White neighborhoods, but buying a single-family home was often still a challenge if not impossible for people of color. A host of issues—land-use regulations, the mortgage process and lingering broker bias, to name just a few—made "fair housing" an elusive pursuit for many African Americans. "Steering" was a common practice, with certain brokers choosing which homes should be shown to prospective buyers based on their skin color. Such brokers were also known to point out the flaws of houses in some areas to Black people while never mentioning such things to Whites, an example that more subtle techniques were being used than in the even more draconian past. The majority of brokers' business came from Whites, and they were careful not to alienate those who were not in favor of integration, even if it cost them a commission from a sale to an African American.[312]

Enjoy It While It Lasts

In addition to serving as an opportunity for racism to foment, the development of Long Island over the past half century came at another significant cost. The early 1970s were a golden age of environmentalism, and the effects of the massive changes to the ecosystem of the island were, deservedly, getting increasing attention. The coastline of the South Shore was of particular concern, as erosion threatened the very existence of the beaches. "Enjoy it while it lasts," warned Stephen R. Davenport Jr. in the *New York Times* in 1972, because next year "it may not be there." The shoreline between Fire Island and Jones Beach was disappearing at a rate of three to four feet a year, which was more significant than it might sound (particularly if you happened to own a house on the beach). The shoreline between Fire Island and East Hampton was eroding at more than twice that rate, making some homeowners sorry they built or bought their house so close to the Atlantic Ocean. The increasing frequency of hurricane-level storms was compounding the problem, another being that there were fewer sand dunes on the beach than there used to be, many having been bulldozed away for homes.[313]

Shana Alexander, a columnist for *Newsweek*, offered her thoughts on what was taking place on the island's East End. "This basically agricultural area is now deeply, perhaps suicidally threatened by massive development," she wrote, as more potato fields were split up into lots or paved over for roads. As well, more marinas for more boats were polluting the shoreline, not good for the remaining oystermen. Current zoning plans were based on economic, aesthetic or sociological interests, but Alexander argued that the environment should come first, or "the golden goose will have died from fouling its own nest." Even if development lowered taxes (which it didn't, the facts showed, as more services had to be provided), continued growth on the East End would ultimately make there no reason for people to want to live or visit there.[314]

While greater interest in such dire warnings was being shown by community planners (talk of drilling for oil in the waters off Montauk raised considerable alarm), it hardly meant that residential development would stop. In fact, a relatively new kind of home—the condominium—was "sprouting in the fertile soil of Long Island," David A. Andelman of *Newsday* noted in 1973, with some developers believing it was "the suburban housing of the future." About fifteen condominium developments were in the works on Long Island (the state attorney general had to approve their go-ahead), making builders of rental apartments rethink their business model.[315]

At about one thousand square feet, the first condos to be built were quite compact by normal housing standards, so it would take some time for home buyers to get used to the idea of living in such a small space. In place of size (and a basement), however, there were typically swimming pools, tennis courts, putting greens and lots of parking spaces, amenities that were attracting younger people with a steady income. Then, as now, tax deductions on mortgage interest payments and possible appreciation were incentives to avoid renting if one could come up with the down payment. But unlike the Long Island house market, which consisted largely of urbanites wanting more space to spread out, most condominium buyers were renters who already lived in Suffolk or Nassau Counties and wanted to start building equity.[316]

As more developers, seeing less and less land on Long Island to turn into affordable housing, saw condominiums as a legitimate alternative to building single-family homes, county planners thought long and hard about how much growth should be allowed take place. Long Island's "master planner" was Lee Koppelman, executive director of the Nassau-Suffolk Regional Planning Board in 1974. While not nearly as powerful as Robert Moses, Koppelman did have considerable say in charting the future course of the island that had a higher population than half the states. "Long Island is America in microcosm," he said, but the former's chaotic growth since the creation of Levittown in the later 1940s was unlike that of most other places. Developers had had too much decision-making power over where to put their building projects, he thought, resulting in too many people and shopping centers in some areas and not enough in others.[317]

To guide his vision, Koppelman had a sixty-volume document called the *Nassau-Suffolk Comprehensive Development Plan*, published in 1970. The first priority of the plan was to preserve open space; just 6.5 percent of the land in Nassau was vacant, and no future development could take place in any remaining woodland or wetland. Of Suffolk County, 41 percent was vacant, a surprising number given how much construction and traffic there was, even at its eastern end. New development in Suffolk could only happen in existing residential, commercial or industrial areas, reinforcing the plan's overriding goal to use vacant land only for agricultural, recreational or conservation purposes.[318]

One might think that with such language in the plan, Long Island had reached its maximum development, but that wasn't the case. There would be more housing, more roads and more people on the island, Koppelman made clear, quite a trick given that none of it could be located in open space. Concentrating the growth in the three *C*s—corridors, clusters and centers—was the key to this sleight of hand, a doable proposition since Koppelman and his bosses (the Nassau Board of Supervisors and the Suffolk legislature) had the power to review zoning regulations and alterations. Such extensive planning was considered necessary given how urban Long Island had become over the years. If there was any doubt of that, the Nassau-Suffolk region had been designated a "standard metropolitan statistical area" by the federal government, the only one in the country that didn't have a core city within its borders.[319] The designation had interesting implications, as David Jacobs wrote in *Newsday*:

> It acknowledges, for the first time officially, that a region adjacent to a city, however great its economic dependence on the city, will now be regarded as an independent physical entity with social, environmental and political characteristics unrelated to the city—characteristics that should be categorized separately from those of the city.[320]

Koppelman's sixty-volume *Nassau-Suffolk Comprehensive Development Plan* seemed to make sense, but some Long Islanders were not waiting around for their quality of life to improve. One man who left Long Island with his family (to live on a farm in Nova Scotia) told his story in *Newsday* in 1974, summing up their decision as "we wanted a better life." Will Graves had a nice government job and lived with his wife and children in a big house in Smithtown, things many could only dream about. It was a seemingly endless traffic jam on Jericho Turnpike on a hot summer day that served as a tipping point of sorts, and Graves swore to himself that he would not be doing that the rest of his life. Life was hard in rural Nova Scotia, but Graves felt very much alive there versus what he described as the "9-to-5, 'Thank-God-it's-Friday' society" of Long Island. And since it was seventy-five miles to the nearest town of any size, there were definitely no traffic jams.[321]

A year and a half later, another story in the same newspaper featured a different set of refugees from Long Island who believed they would be happier somewhere else. This time it was the Phelan family, who were moving from East Meadow to Phoenix, Arizona, not to avoid traffic jams but to get a lot more for their money. The young couple had certainly run the numbers, finding that a brand new four-bedroom house in the desert with a pool and wall-to-wall carpeting (it was the 1970s, after all) would cost $48,000, a better deal than buying a preowned two-bedroom house in a bad neighborhood on Long Island for $30,000. As well, taxes were much lower in Phoenix, and there would be no snow to shovel or occasional hurricane from which to flee. Mrs. Phelan grew up in Levittown but had no sentimental attachment to the place.[322]

Home builders all over the country knew that in the current economic climate, less would be more. Just as auto makers were shrinking their models to offer consumers cheaper, more fuel-efficient cars, the housing industry was downsizing dwellings to make them more affordable for the battered middle class. Americans had also realized they didn't need all the extras that typically came with a new house, ready to give up a family room and garage if it meant the ability to own something rather than rent. The condo market had not taken off as expected, more reason to make one-family homes within reach of average earners. The typical new house in the New York metropolitan area cost $55,000, but the no frills version sold by the builder Kaufman and Broad near Islip went for $35,000, a huge difference during the recent recession and energy crisis.[323]

A NEW ETHIC

Small or large houses aside, many believed that suburbia itself was a broken model by the nation's bicentennial. Because there was no central core of Long Island, as there typically was in most urban areas (often called downtown), the island (divided into two counties) was a fragmented mosaic or patchwork quilt of hundreds of townships, villages and what were called special districts. (Two communities in Nassau County— Glen Cove and Long Beach—qualified as cities.) This makeup of Long Island was, for many, confusing and disorienting, as it was difficult to get an authentic sense of place if one lived, worked, shopped and socialized in different communities, as many residents did. As well, this was an inefficient way to run local government services, as there was significant overlap (and often contention) among all the different communities. "The communities remain little islands, each jealously guarding in particular its zoning powers as if they were divine rights," Samuel Kaplan wrote in his book *The Dream Deferred*; his own town of Port Washington as balkanized as any on Long Island.[324]

Given Kaplan's take on the state of Long Island, it could be seen how a sixty-volume development plan was required to address its many problems. "Unfocused regional growth, uncoordinated public service, fossilized local governments and economic and racial discrimination" were some of those problems, he wrote, and that wasn't even mentioning tax disparities. Many Long Islanders were at least partly aware of at least some of the major challenges in their—and/or surrounding—town or village but, understandably, felt there was little or nothing they (or perhaps anyone) could do about them. "New structures, if not a new ethic, are needed if the American dream of the good life is to be fulfilled," Kaplan stated. "Suburbia has tested our institutions and found them wanting."

Kaplan certainly made good points about suburbia in the 1970s, but America's cities were hardly paradises at the time. New York City was in especially deep trouble as the tall ships sailed into the Hudson River to celebrate the bicentennial, as both people and jobs left for greener pastures. (President Ford never actually said, "Drop dead," as the now-infamous 1975 headline in the *Daily News* read, but his refusal to provide federal assistance to save New York from bankruptcy was real.)[325] Michael Drew was one of those people who left New York for the greater career opportunities to be found on Long Island and the possibility of becoming a homeowner. "As the city sinks, as the jobs leave for the suburbs or more exotic locations that offer plenty of sunshine and non-union labor, people like me have to go where the jobs are," he explained in *Newsday*. Drew left the city to take a solid job on Long Island and, through a stroke of good luck, was able to buy a small house in Lake Ronkonkoma in which to raise his growing family.[326]

With an average income, Drew was indeed lucky to become a homeowner. (He had made a private deal with the sellers, as no bank would have offered him a mortgage.)[327] The median cost of a house in the United States in 1976 was $46,000, which was about twice what it had been in 1970 because of galloping inflation. Coming up with the down payment and qualifying for a mortgage was just the beginning, however. Mortgage payments, fuel (oil for heating on Long Island, likely—not a good thing given current relations with OPEC countries), electricity (LILCO was known as one of the priciest utilities nationwide), property taxes and repairs and insurance were ongoing costs, and those didn't include the addition of that deck or white picket fence one thought would make the house complete. Salaries had gone up but not proportionately to the cost of living, making homeownership on Long Island and in most of the rest of the country a challenging pursuit for anyone but the rich.[328]

With fewer prospective buyers, home building had slowed down dramatically on Long Island and throughout the Northeast, triggering high rates of unemployment in construction—a major source of jobs. Some trade unions had cut their rates to try to stir up work for their members, but it wasn't enough to make much of a difference. Tinkering with mortgage payments was another way to jump-start home building and buying. A fluctuating variable rate mortgage was one new formula, a graduated rate mortgage another, which increased as borrowers' income rose over time. While those could be helpful, only a more systematic program, such as government-subsidized housing for low- and moderate-income families (one of presidential candidate Jimmy Carter's campaign platforms) would kick-start a solution to the rather dismal housing situation on Long Island.[329]

Some middle-income Long Islanders who already owned a home were renting out part of it to another family to make much-needed extra cash, something not quite legal in most towns and villages. Communities on the island were generally zoned exclusively for single-family residences, a means to limit congestion and use of strained public services. A growing number of landlords were receiving summons for violating the law, creating considerable contention between them and local administrations. Mineola officials were being especially tough on homeowners with tenants, but the former defended their position by pointing out the extra garbage to be picked up, more water used and, perhaps, more crowded schools without additional real estate taxes being paid. The practice had been going on since before World War II, but budget cuts were encouraging towns like Mineola to crack down.[330]

The even worse news for prospective homeowners was that experts were predicting it would become even more difficult to get a piece of the American dream. By 1981, according to a report by the Harvard-MIT Joint Center for Urban Studies, it would cost $78,000 to buy a typical median-priced new house, far out of reach for most Americans, including Long Islanders. The average price of a preowned house on the island in 1976 was $42,000, and even that was too pricey for the majority of renters. Property taxes on Long Island were among the highest in the country, additional reason for such folks to not go house hunting. The only good news seemed to be that more married women were working full time, creating more households with dual incomes. Bankers had been asking women what kind of birth control they were using when deciding if a couple should get a mortgage (presumably to learn if there would be another mouth to feed in the family), but laws had recently banned that odious practice.[331]

Given the scenario of homeownership on Long Island in the late '70s, was it any wonder that some were considering alternatives to the standard one-family house? One cheaper alternative was a mobile home, an abode that also offered significantly lower maintenance costs than a house. Those who were living on fixed incomes but also wanted some sense of community were gravitating to mobile-home parks like one in East Quogue or the Glenwood Adult Leisure Community in Riverhead. There were actually thirty-six such parks in Suffolk County, although the price of living in them was also going up due to escalating space rental fees. Still, mobile homes enabled those with low or moderate income to own a piece of property and even tend a small garden without having to mow a lawn. Many older mobile home owners in Suffolk had downsized from a house to cut costs, although some young married couples were also finding them to be good starter homes. It was easier to get a mortgage for a mobile home, but interest payments were higher, as the lower prices made it possible to pay the mortgage back faster. Like condos a few years back, mobile homes were said by some to be the "housing of the future," but anti-sprawlers were hoping that wouldn't be the case.[332]

By 1977, however, the country had pulled out of the recession, allowing more people to invest in what Robert Lindsey of the *New York Times* called "the traditional American dream house—the detached home on its own lot." Housing construction was up nationwide, including on Long Island, good news for local economies. The miniboom was being driven by baby boomer DINKs—dual-income no kids couples—as well as single people making good money. Unlike their Depression-era parents, boomers were not averse to going into major debt if that's what it took to get a place of their own. The days of putting one hundred dollars down to own a house were long over, but that wasn't going to stop thirtysomethings on the fast track to buying into the classic American way of life after their rebellious youth.[333]

The Busy-ness Syndrome

Running parallel with the advent of more working women in the 1970s was the feminist movement. The plight of the "suburban woman" was one of the themes of the movement, as she was widely considered to be decidedly unliberated, stuck in her traditional gender role as housewife and homemaker. Making the rounds of Long Island libraries in the fall of 1977 was a series of lectures dedicated to the theme of women in the suburbs, with no fewer than eighty talks (!) given by thirty scholars from disparate fields. The goal of this series was to help suburban women "improve their lives," although it wasn't quite clear that the women wanted their lives improved. Susan Pashman, the Adelphi University philosophy professor who organized the talks, saw them as a consciousness-raising of sorts—i.e., an effort to make the women more aware of themselves from a social and political perspective. After laying the groundwork, Pashman envisioned suburban women making real changes to find greater contentedness in their lives.[334]

The free series of talks taking place at more than sixteen Long Island libraries was indeed eclectic, with lectures on topics including the historical role of suburban women, going to work, creativity, psychoanalysis, the future of marriage and "new lifestyles." Pashman's own talk, titled "The Waxy Yellow Build-Up" (a reference to a Pledge furniture cleaner commercial that was hilariously co-opted in an episode of the television show *Mary Hartman, Mary Hartman*), addressed how advertising presented suburbia as a kind of utopia. "Suburban women are led to believe that they have attained the American Dream, and how dare they be disgruntled with or criticize a lifestyle that epitomizes utopia?" she told a reporter for the *New York Times*. Not too surprisingly, Pashman had left Long Island, finding the suburbs hostile to single parents like herself.[335]

Other speakers in the series tried to find reasons to be upbeat about the position of women in suburban societies like Long Island. Susan Squier, who taught English at SUNY Stony Brook, wondered why modern women writers almost always located female protagonists in the city rather than the suburbs. As well, writing about the suburbs by women authors tended to be polarized—i.e., humorous (Erna Bombeck, Judith Viorst) or depressing (Sylvia Plath). Squier believed there could be more constructive approaches within the genre of suburban literature. One other lecturer was Michael D'Innocenzo, a history professor at Hofstra, who addressed marriage, family and gender roles in suburbia. Going against the grain, D'Innocenzo was optimistic about the role of women in the 'burbs despite the many challenges they currently faced, which included their domestic containment, the "intimacy deprivation" encouraged by commuting and "the busy-ness syndrome" of everyday life. The feminist movement, later marriages, fewer children and greater acceptance of singlehood were reasons why the professor felt good about the future of women in the suburbs.[336]

Feminists like Pashman, however, were not about to stick around Long Island while such sociological trends took root. It wasn't just feminists leaving the island in the late 1970s, however. Young adults viewed Long Island much differently than their parents, many of whom considered it a paradise for raising a family when they relocated from the city in the 1950s. For someone in their twenties, however, the island could easily be seen as a not very challenging and stifling place, with a lack of good jobs and a too high cost of living. Taxes, if nothing else, were driving many young adults off the island, triggering a wholesale change in its culture. Long Island was literally built around the institution of marriage, the raising of children, and women's primary role as housewives—all things that were in great flux in the late '70s. Accelerating congestion, economic stagnation, a heavily automotive-centric transportation system and overdevelopment of the natural environment had, over the past two decades, contributed to the recent population decline, with more outflow from the island than inflow from New York City.[337]

Looking to the future, academics and planners could see that Long Island would have to adapt to a different set of economic and social conditions if it wasn't to become a lesser version of New York City. Retaining the essence of the island within the context of slower growth and an aging population appeared to be the key for it to thrive in the years ahead. Both spouses having to work in order to pay the bills was certainly not the case in the postwar era and something that conservatives worried might break up the traditional family. (The divorce rate was indeed up.) Research suggested that concerns about a mass migration of young people from the island were justified. A 1978 survey of seniors at two Long Island high schools by *Newsday* revealed that 73 percent of those polled did not intend to settle in the area, citing limited job opportunities and the high cost of living as the primary reasons for their plans to eventually move to parts unknown. Much of Long Island's aerospace industry was gone, and building more homes didn't seem like an exciting career for most seventeen-year-olds.[338]

One didn't have to be an expert to notice how much of the social landscape of Long Island had changed since the Eisenhower administration. Some of the schools that were hurriedly built as the generation to be known as baby boomers went through their childhood were now closing, Little League participation was down and even visits to Santa Claus at Roosevelt Field had dramatically shrunk. Most significantly, community life remained largely steeped in the needs and interests of the nuclear family despite the rise of single and divorced people. Many felt increasingly isolated, not a good thing for growing or even maintaining the population. Even though boomers currently ranged between their late teens and early thirties, there were already concerns about the economic and other implications of an elderly society. (A decrease in crime was one of the few projected benefits of there being a greater number of older people in a few decades.) "This is the decade of the urban crisis," stated Richard Wade, an urban historian at CUNY. "The 1980s will be the decade of the suburban crisis."[339]

Those thinking Long Island no longer matched their lifestyle could be in for a rude surprise when they tried to sell their house. The Bindrims of Setauket, for example, wanted to move to Connecticut, where they could get more land for less money and pay lower taxes. (Of those planning to move from Long Island, 90 percent were set on moving out of state, a 1978 *Newsday* poll showed.) There were no takers for the list price of $61,000, however, and still no offers when they dropped the price by $10,000. After hearing from their broker that the four-bedroom home wouldn't sell even if they dropped the price by another $10,000 because of the glut of similar houses in Suffolk, the Bindrims decided to stay put. While the buyer's market for preowned houses was good for entry-level homeowners, the economics ran contrary to the general principle that property appreciated in value. Homeowners were literally banking on their house to increase in value over time, not just to keep up with inflation but also to fund a nest egg for their children's college or retirement.[340]

The case of the Bindrims was not unusual and clear evidence that Long Island was in an economic slump. Civil servants from New York City had long comprised a large percentage of Long Island home buyers, but that market had mostly dried up as companies on the island departed and the cost of gas and commuter train tickets went up. A renter could now get a used house relatively cheaply on Long Island, but that proposition had become less attractive as the downsides magnified. As well, while a good deal, a $50,000 house still required a down payment of what it would have cost to buy a new house in Levittown outright in the late 1940s, and the monthly carrying costs were far greater, even when adjusted for inflation. Long Island now had the highest property taxes in the country—three to four times the national average.[341] Running such numbers, Long Island developers were themselves relocating to places like Dallas, Atlanta or even Chicago, where property taxes were significantly lower.[342]

In such an adverse real estate environment, was it any surprise that many Long Island builders were offering juicy incentives to move their product? The cost of new homes may have been low, especially in Suffolk, but property taxes were exorbitant relative to the price, not a good model to appeal to the bread-and-butter market of moderate-income families. Free closing costs or at-no-cost appliances were a couple of deals being offered to make a sale, with attractive interest rates and cash rebates other perks. But with the high rate of unemployment on Long Island and the distinct possibility that one's own job could go west, south or all the way to Japan, even these often weren't capable of motivating most middle-class renters to sign on the dotted line.[343]

Living Without the Dream

For many residents of and visitors to the Hamptons, such concerns were inconsequential. Largely unspoiled—unlike most of the rest of Long Island, many would say—the villages remained a seasonal outpost among a certain set of New Yorkers. Attracted to the light and quiet, artists had occupied the East End since the 1920s, but by the late 1970s, the literati had claimed it as their turf. F. Scott Fitzgerald's ghost could still be found in the Hamptons; the beach house once owned by Sara and Gerald Murphy, who had served as models for Nicole and Dick Diver in *Tender Is the Night*, had recently been the site of a party held for John Updike and his new wife. Truman Capote, Joseph Heller, Shana Alexander and George Plimpton were regulars on the Hamptons party circuit, and Edward Albee's annual party in Montauk had already become legendary, with guests including Lee Radziwill, Ben Bradlee, Sally Quinn and Katherine Graham. Bobby Van's bar in Bridgehampton was writers' favorite hangout, and Elaine Steinbeck (John's widow) was still very much a presence in Sag Harbor.[344]

One might have found the popular novelist Susan Isaacs at Bobby Van's, but she was more often seen in or around her home in Manhasset. Interestingly, when Isaacs became somewhat famous after one of her more successful books was published, her friends and neighbors routinely asked when she was departing the town for more glamorous digs. Isaacs found this odd, since she believed that Nassau County was a great place for a novelist to live. While hardly chic, Manhasset was "normal" and populated by polite people who left her alone to write. But as she grew up in Brooklyn and Queens, the North Shore of Long Island was, for Isaacs, quite a leap. "The move east, to Nassau County, was simply a normal step up, another rung scaled on the social ladder," she explained in *Newsday* in 1978—a long way from her grandparents' move from a Polish shtetl to a Lower East Side tenement. It may have been a cliché and outdated, but Isaacs's split-level house, complete with marriage and kids, was her American dream, a refreshing view given all the bad news being assigned to Long Island. "I find myself intimidated by the pressures of Manhattan, by its intellectual rigors, its perfectly cosmeticized faces, its well-cut suits and epigrams," she confessed.[345]

A stone's throw or so from Isaac's home sweet home in Manhasset was North Hills, where a major condominium project called the Estates was going up. With no unit less than $132,000 ($542,000 today), the Estates targeted specifically "upper-income people," a nod to the fact that the Grace, Paley and Whitney families all still had places in the area. In 1975, the developer had bought the eighty-acre plot from the New York Society of the Province of Jesus, and the Jesuits retained some twenty acres and their turn-of-the-century mansion in the center of the Estates. The aesthetic of the development was inspired by "the California look," something new to Long Island that seemed to appeal to the wealthy buyers.[346]

Prices of homes in California were skyrocketing at the tail end of the 1970s, part of the reason why "upper-income people" on Long Island wanted their condos to look like they were shipped in from Newport Beach. While a flat economy was not conducive to creating jobs, it was keeping a lid on home prices on Long Island, something that couldn't be said of places like Orange County, the Bay Area, the Washington, D.C. suburbs and Greenwich, Connecticut. Like America as a whole, Long Island real estate was getting increasingly polarized, with homes in the Hamptons and on the North Shore at the upper end of the spectrum and tract houses in central Suffolk at the bottom. Long Island had a very diverse population in terms of income, and the housing market clearly reflected the growing divide between the haves and have-nots.[347] The have-nots were spending as much of their income as possible to buy a home, seeing ownership as the best possible hedge against inflation.[348]

If the haves had their way, the have-nots would not be their neighbors. The class and racial divide on Long Island could be detected in the widespread resistance against federally subsidized housing for low-income residents. Rezoning was often required to build such housing, sometimes turning public hearings to discuss proposed projects into shouting matches between the yeas and the nays. Timothy J. McInerny, editor of the *Suffolk Home Builder*, was surprised at the level of what he called "middle-class provincialism" (and "parochialism") during these hearings; urbanites who had moved to Long Island years back were typically against providing affordable housing for those who now wanted to make the same journey. There were the "wes" and the "theys," the former determined to prevent the latter from moving into their town or village lest it become a slum in the making. McInerney labeled this the "keep-out syndrome," hardly exclusive to Long Island but a common condition in both Suffolk and Nassau Counties nonetheless.[349]

In the case of African Americans, Long Island's keep-out syndrome could take forms far more nefarious than loud squabbles at town hearings. Just as the unloading of drugs on Long Island's beaches was a throwback to Prohibition-era rum-running, destruction of Blacks' property and other hate crimes was reminiscent of the past. In 1979, Thomas Mosely of Deer Park got a phone call informing him that his house was on fire, and the man had a gut feeling that it was the work of arsonists. Mosely's suspicions were right, as the previous day, he had noticed ashes in the shape of a cross on the front lawn. Mosely had reported the incident to police and asked for greater security to protect the house, but as in the past in similar cases, that didn't seem to have happened. Mosely and his family were living in an apartment in Brooklyn and, like many city dwellers, planned to move to Long Island to become homeowners.[350]

Although the only part of the house still standing was the front wall, the Moselys were determined to start over. "We were just going to let it go but when we actually saw it, we were so angry we decided to build again," Mosely told the *New York Amsterdam News*. Given what had taken place, the family was surprised to find strong community support, with neighbors doing what they could to help out. As well, a fundraiser for the Moselys was planned by the Deer Park First Baptist Church and the local civic association. (The insurance company was, however, another matter; its representatives argued that since a wall was left standing, the house could be repaired. The company also offered to pay just five months of living expenses rather than the twelve months specified in Mosely's contract.) When the Moselys had looked at the property during an open house, the realtors had told them that race would not be an issue. Calls from the Moselys to the realtors were unreturned.[351]

The burning of the Moselys' house was not an isolated incident. There had been at least two other criminal destructions of African Americans' homes in Suffolk in the previous six months, cause for some kind of legal action to be taken to try to prevent more from taking place. Hank Johnston, executive director of the Suffolk County Human Rights Commission, met with leaders from a number of Black organizations and county officials to raise awareness of the persistent problem. One meeting was with the Long Island Board of Realtors to discuss new legislation to protect minorities, and Johnston also asked the United States Justice Department to investigate the cases.[352]

There was some complicated backstory to the Mosely case related to Kaplan's concern about the geographic fragmentation of Long Island. The family's house in Deer Park was located in a hamlet within the town of Babylon, a community that, a few years earlier, rejected construction of a low- to middle-income housing development in nearby Wyandanch. (Wyandanch was one of oldest and largest African American communities on Long Island.) Residents of Deer Park were strongly against the building of that development, fearing that it could lower property values in their area, with racial attitudes also no doubt in play.[353]

Sadly, six months later, another cross burning at the home of an African American family took place on Long Island, this one in North Valley Stream. A week earlier, a rock was thrown through the front window of Inga Grant's home, which she shared with her seven children. There had been other cross burnings in the area and some firebombings that were clearly racially motivated, although police described the acts as "youthful pranks." Long Island civil rights leaders again called for formal investigations into the incidents and prosecution of those charged. In the Grant case, two men were arrested for both the rock throwing and cross burning; the men, who lived in a White area of North Valley Stream, were charged with criminal mischief and harassment.[354]

While African Americans faced their own, especially virulent, obstacles to realizing their American dream of owning a home, it was clear by the end of the 1970s that many Long Islanders would find such a thing a highly elusive pursuit. In a piece titled "Living Without the Dream," published eleven days before the end of the decade, Jerry Morgan of *Newsday* offered a glimpse of the challenges that lay ahead for prospective homeowners. "The 1980s will be a tough time for those building, buying, selling, and seeking housing on Long Island," the newspaper's real estate writer posited, a much different story than what would have been envisioned in decades past. Construction issues (i.e., caps on growth and environmental and zoning restrictions as well as the high cost of materials and land) "may make the single-family house all but unattainable except for the affluent," Morgan fretted, predicting far fewer new home permits would be taken out in the foreseeable future.[355]

Construction was just a part of the real estate puzzle, however, and only one reason why many Long Islanders would be living without the dream in the '80s, Morgan believed. Water supply on the island was a major problem, suggesting that any new housing would be clustered close together to preserve open land. As well, both residents and local governments now often opposed zoning changes for new housing, and up-front costs had become too high for most developers anyway. Morgan was not sanguine about what had long been the primary reason for people to choose Long Island as a place to live. "The American Dream of a new, single-family house on its own lot began to fade in the 1970s," he observed, "and we will begin to learn to live without it in the 1980s."[356] Morgan's prediction would prove prophetic, as it became increasingly clear that the golden days of Long Island resided in its past.

CONCLUSION

Did Jerry Morgan's prediction about the 1980s being a tough time for realizing the classic American dream of single-family homeownership turn out to be true? It certainly appeared to, as home prices continued to spiral upward, putting the dream out of reach for most of those with an average income. "Have we awakened from the 'Long Island Dream?'" asked W.D. Wetherell in *Newsday* in 1981. According to him, its achievability in the United States had shifted decidedly southwest to the Sun Belt.[357] The continual shortage of affordable housing on Long Island, as in other suburban areas across the country, was in stark contrast to what the middle class had experienced from the 1920s through the 1960s. To make matters worse, a recession in the early '80s triggered a spike in bankruptcies on the island, and house foreclosures were rampant. Meanwhile, wealthy investors, some of them foreign, were scooping up remaining prime real estate on the East End, dividing Long Island further into the haves and have-nots. The media was fascinated by the time's yuppie phenomenon, but it was clear that average baby boomers didn't have it nearly as good as their parents. Also unlike their parents, most middle-aged Long Islanders now worked in the bi-county area, making the connection to New York City far weaker than it had once been.

On Long Island and elsewhere, it could be safely said that the American dream had effectively shrunk as expectations for what was economically feasible or practical were lowered. Condominiums became an increasingly popular housing option and a more reachable version of homeownership.

Smaller cars offering more miles to the gallon appeared on the island's roads, their fuel economy far superior to that of the giant gas guzzlers. Two-career couples multiplied in number as it became evident that a single paycheck was no longer enough to support a high-overhead lifestyle. (For some, part of that high overhead was going to cocaine, a drug reportedly ubiquitous on Long Island in the 1980s.) Relaxed zoning codes and subsidized moderate-cost housing were a couple of things some towns were doing to make homeownership possible for the middle class, but local government could only do so much. Most simply, the cost of living on Long Island (especially taxes and utility rates) was significantly higher than the national average, a fact that made itself felt not just in financial terms but in emotional ones as well, judging by the stress many residents were reporting. Bad-as-ever traffic jams and a lack of career opportunities served as other major drawbacks to the place a previous generation considered a virtual paradise. Young adults who had happily grown up on the island were realizing that it was no longer an ideal location to settle down and have kids and were looking instead to places like California, Florida or, most shockingly, Jersey. Billy Joel, perhaps Long Island's most famous resident, made it clear he wasn't going anywhere, but more and more of his fans were as, one of his songs went, "movin' out."

By the end of the twentieth century, it was readily apparent that much of Long Island had become unacceptably crowded and expensive—precisely the same reasons why previous generations had moved there from New York City. Adding and improving roads had been a big part of the island's development, but now some were concluding that the only solution was for people to drive less. (Spoiler alert: the proposed span across Long Island Sound was never built, deemed literally a bridge too far. Talk of a thirty-mile tunnel between Long Island and Connecticut could be heard in the early 2000s, but the estimated cost of at least $3 billion squashed that idea.) Homeownership remained an elusive pursuit for many Long Islanders through the 1990s; in fact, Levittown became historically landmarked, an apt symbol of the American dream now being in the rearview mirror for much of the middle class. As well, thousands of defense-contracting jobs had disappeared over the years, putting a major dent in the local economy.[358]

Despite a decline in quality of life, however, the classic suburban lifestyle steeped in neighborhoods, backyards and good schools could still be found on Long Island, and both the beach and the Big Apple were not that far away. Could the deferred American dream make a comeback? Perhaps, but if so, it was likely to be a significantly more multicultural one. Once the province of the White middle class, Long Island had, by the 1990s, become much more racially, ethnically and economically heterogenous, more accurately reflecting the diversity of the United States. Hispanic and Asian immigrants arrived in great numbers in the last decades of the twentieth century, reshaping the demographic contours of the island. More than any other institution, the National Center for Suburban Studies at Hofstra University has recognized and celebrated this evolution of diversity on Long Island; the center is strongly committed to addressing the social inequities that have defined suburban communities in the United States.[359] To that point, Long Island remains heavily racially segregated, a legacy of its Jim Crow past, with discrimination based on skin color persisting to this day. On a more positive note, single moms (and some dads) are no longer considered outsiders, a function of the startlingly high divorce rate and more liberal attitudes of the last few decades. As well, the LGBT community is a visible presence on Long Island today, more evidence that the island has become more inclusive.

The year 2000 appeared to be a turning point in the history of Long Island, as it became clear that its twentieth century model of development was no longer relevant or useful. Entering a new century and new millennium seemingly encouraged Long Islanders to imagine a different kind of American dream than their economically fortunate parents had enjoyed. In an ironic twist, the tech boom was turning one of the original reasons to move to the island upside down. Some start-ups were being based on Long Island for the more affordable office space to be had (and due to 9/11) but were located near train stations, so employees living in the city could easily reverse commute. Many young adults, even those who grew up on the island, were continuing to choose to live in hipper urban neighborhoods (where one didn't need to own a car). That, combined with the graying of baby boomers, was raising the average age of Long Islanders, a concern for many communities facing the prospect of lower tax revenues and higher public expenditures. The subprime mortgage mess and widened gap between the rich and poor only exacerbated such concerns and made many nostalgically long for the idealized halcyon days of the 1950s. On the surface, the island may have looked much the same in the early twenty-first century as it did during the Eisenhower administration, but the fact was that it had become a much different place.

Today, rather happily, the cultural ecosystem of Long Island and its built environment are being reexamined in light of concepts such as new urbanism, smart growth, the green movement and sustainable neighborhoods. The days of Robert Moses are clearly over, as planners reimagine the possibilities of suburban life with its dependence on cars and lack of communal interaction (save for that at shopping malls). More bike paths have popped up, and reducing one's carbon footprint has become a primary goal among many concerned about global warming, suggesting that the island is in the process of being "remade." Still, Long Island was developed on a much different set of principles than those in currency today, presenting a major challenge in terms of its long-term viability as a good place to live both today and tomorrow. All in all, however, much of the island's natural beauty and original appeal remain, offering hope that a new and improved American dream can and will emerge in the years ahead.

NOTES

Introduction

1. For pre-twentieth-century histories of Long Island, see Gabriel, *Evolution of Long Island*; Overton, *Long Island's Story*; Jackson, *Stories of Long Island*; Pennypacker, *General Washington's Spies*; Sealock and Seely, *Long Island Bibliography*; Dyson, *Anecdotes and Events*; Dyson, *Human Story of Long Island*; and Krieg, *Long Island Studies*.
2. Panchyk, *Hidden History*, 9, 59.
3. Ibid., 55, 57, 63; For more on the history of the LIRR, see Smith and Friedman, *Long Island R.R.*; Seyfried, *Long Island Railroad*; and Fischer, *Long Island Rail Road*. See also the Long Island Rail Road Collection at Long Island Studies Institute Collections at Hofstra University (LISIC).
4. See Kaiser, Stonier and Discalla, *Aerospace Industry on Long Island*; Stoff, *Aerospace Heritage of Long Island*; Stoff, *From Airship to Spaceship*; and Shodell, *Flight of Memory*.
5. Panchyk, *Hidden History*, 17, 28, 31, 66, 74.
6. Ibid., 83, 105. See Sobin, *Long Island's Declining "Gold Coast."*
7. See Samuel, *American Dream*.
8. See Gans, *Levittowners*; Kelly, *Expanding the American Dream*; Ferrer and Navarra, *Levittown*; and Kushner, *Levittown*. See also the William J. Levitt and Simone Korchin Levitt Scrapbook (LISIC).

9. For more on Long Island as the quintessential suburban Long Island experience, see Kelly, *Suburban Experience*; Kelly, *Suburbia Re-Examined*; and Silver and Melkonian, *Contested Terrain*.

10. See Caro, *Power Broker*, and Krieg, *Single-Minded Genius*. See also the Jones Beach Collection and the Long Island Parkways Collection (LISIC).

11. See Day, *African Americans on Long Island*, and Naylor, *Long Island and Beyond*. See also the African Americans on Long Island Collection (LISIC).

Chapter 1

12. P.H. Woodward, "Observations of Long Island Seer," *New-York Tribune*, April 22, 1923.

13. Quinn L. Martin, "Long Island Society Will Be 'Up in the Air' This Summer," *New-York Tribune*, April 11, 1920.

14. "Merrick Road Reported in Fairly Good Shape," *New-York Tribune*, May 11, 1920.

15. "You Can Drive 200 Miles on Good Long Island Roads," *New-York Tribune*, July 25, 1920.

16. "Extreme Eastern End of Long Island Is Tour's Objective," *New-York Tribune*, August 7, 1921.

17. "Long Island Ready for Gay Autumn Season," *New-York Tribune*, September 8, 1920.

18. "How Long Island's Million Acres Are Utilized," *New-York Tribune*, January 9, 1921.

19. "Passports for Long Island?" *New-York Tribune*, April 22, 1921.

20. "16,697 Families Built Homes on Long Island Last Year," *New-York Tribune*, February 19, 1922.

21. "Active Lot Market in Near-by Suburbs," *New York Times*, October 8, 1922.

22. "Booming Long Island," *New York Times*, November 12, 1922.

23. "500 Long Island Acres Bought for Small Home Sites," *New-York Tribune*, February 18, 1923.

24. "Long Island Hotels Begin Campaign to Win More Visitors," *New-York Tribune*, April 6, 1922.

25. "Rum Smugglers Stir Many Towns," *New York Times*, March 17, 1923.

26. Ibid.

27. "Plan War on Bootleggers," *New York Times*, July 7, 1923.

28. "Want 4 New Roads for Long Island," *New York Times*, July 15, 1923.

29. "Commuters Find a Paradise in Rockville Center and Lynbrook," *New-York Tribune*, August 26, 1923.

30. "'Hub of Long Island' Is Name Given to Beautiful Hempstead," *New-York Tribune*, September 16, 1923.

31. "Klan Rule of Politics Feared on Long Island," *New-York Tribune*, September 19, 1923.

32. "Klansmen Join U.S. Agents in Liquor Seizure," *New York Herald Tribune*, March 21, 1924.

33. "Coast Guard Acts to Close Cabaret 15 Miles Out at Sea," *New York Times*, August 17, 1924.

34. "'Big House' Territory Is Rapidly Giving Way to Small Houses," *New York Herald Tribune*, November 9, 1924.

35. Ibid.

36. Ibid.

37. "Long Island R.R. Plans Big Changes," *New York Times*, April 4, 1924.

38. "Passenger Growth 2,000,000 in Year," *New York Times*, April 14, 1925.

39. "Plan Belts Roads for Long Island," *New York Times*, May 9, 1925.

40. Edwin A. Osborne, "New Housing Drives Out Long Island Wild Life," *New York Times*, April 5, 1925.

41. "Long Island, Land of Sunshine, Wins Many Families from City," *New York Herald Tribune*, June 7, 1925.

42. Ibid.

43. "The Long Island Park Muddle," *New York Herald Tribune*, September 12, 1925. See *Report of the Long Island State Park Commission* (New York: The Commission, 1925).

44. "Smith Calls State to Fight Rich Few as Park Plan Foes," *New York Times*, June 12, 1925; "A Danger to Long Island," *New York Herald Tribune*, October 25, 1925.

45. "End of Long Island on a Quiet Boom," *New York Times*, October 21, 1925.

46. Ibid.

47. "Long Island's Realty Future Not in Doubt," *New York Herald Tribune*, April 18, 1926.

48. "Real Estate Trading Active along Backbone of Long Island," *New York Herald Tribune*, May 9, 1926.

49. Mildred Adams, "Long Island Has Its Own Land Boom," *New York Times*, June 20, 1926.

50. Ibid.

51. "Tell World About Long Island Has Been Copyrighted," *New York Herald Tribune*, June 27, 1926.

52. "Demands for Homes Has Not Slackened in New York Zone," *New York Herald Tribune*, October 26, 1926.

53. Stacey C. Leech, "Survey Shows Big Demand for Suburbs," *New York Herald Tribune*, April 3, 1927.

54. "Poor Rail Service Stifles Long Island Growth, Board Told," *New York Herald Tribune*, June 24, 1927.

55. "Long Island Highways Built for Big Volume of Traffic," *New York Herald Tribune*, July 24, 1927.

56. "Hasten Work on Long Island New Highway," *New York Herald Tribune*, July 31, 1927.

57. "Progress on Parks Told to Governor," *New York Times*, August 15, 1927.

58. "Long Island Has Grown Faster Than Spain, Italy, Ireland," *New York Herald Tribune*, November 6, 1927.

59. Edmund J. McGrath, "Period of Stability in Long Island Area," *New York Times*, January 8, 1928.

60. "Remote Corners of World 'Interested' in Realty Here," *New York Herald Tribune*, March 18, 1928.

61. "Market Situation on Long Island," *New York Times*, April 29, 1928.

62. "Civic Leader Discuss Future of Long Island," *New York Herald Tribune*, May 2, 1928.

63. "Shore Highway on Long Island to Open Today," *New York Herald Tribune*, June 8, 1929; "Long Island Opens Sunrise Highway," *New York Times*, June 9, 1929.

Chapter 2

64. "Mrs. Mary Kellis's Rites Today: Centenarian Long Island Indian," *New York Herald Tribune*, April 22, 1936. See John A. Strong, *Algonquian Peoples of Long Island from Earliest Times to 1700* (Interlaken, NY: Heart of the Lakes Publishing, 1997); and John A. Strong, *"We Are Still Here!": The Algonquian Peoples of Long Island Today* (Interlaken, NY: Heart of the Lakes Publishing, 1998).

65. "Long Island Development," *New York Times*, February 23, 1930. See R.B. Fernhead, *Long Island: The Sunrise Home Land—Islandwide Survey of Communities, 1929* (New York: Long Island Chamber of Commerce, 1929).

66. "Trip for Run of a Day Given on Long Island," *New York Herald Tribune*, March 9, 1930.

67. "Traffic Needs on Long Island Analyzed by Clubwomen," *New York Herald Tribune*, April 6, 1930.

68. "Parks, Bathing Beaches, Roads for Long Island," *New York Herald Tribune*, April 13, 1930.

69. "History Helps Land Sales on Long Island," *New York Herald Tribune*, May 18, 1930.

70. "Frederick Tells of $50 Lot Days on Long Island," *New York Herald Tribune*, May 25, 1930.

71. "Aviation Has Been Boon to Realty Values," *New York Herald Tribune*, September 21, 1930.

72. "Progressed More in Last Decade Than in Previous Three Centuries," *New York Herald Tribune*, March 20, 1932.

73. "Era of Activity in Long Island Realty Predicted," *New York Herald Tribune*, August 24, 1930.

74. "Beautiful Trails Join Large Estates through Long Island," *New York Herald Tribune*, July 12, 1930.

75. "Long Island Readies for Growing Traffic," *New York Times*, January 4, 1931.

76. William L. Austin, "Values along Seashore Have Moved Upward," *New York Herald Tribune*, January 25, 1931.

77. "Sees Rapid Growth for Long Island," *New York Times*, January 25, 1931.

78. "Families Are Pushing East on Long Island," *New York Herald Tribune*, March 22, 1931.

79. "Private Estate Retreat Before Growth of City," *New York Herald Tribune*, September 27, 1931.

80. "Veteran Clerk Recalls Whaling on Long Island," *New York Herald Tribune*, October 5, 1931. For more on Roosevelt on Long Island, see Natalie A. Naylor, Douglas Brinkley and John Allen Gable, eds., *Theodore Roosevelt: Many-Sided American* (Interlaken, NY: Heart of the Lakes Publishing, 1992).

81. Robert Moses, "Hordes from the City," *Saturday Evening Post*, October 31, 1931.

82. "Long Island Parks Show Income Gain," *New York Times*, April 1, 1932.

83. "Chamber Finds Situation Good on Long Island," *New York Herald Tribune*, April 2, 1932.

84. "Lack of Money for Building Termed Peril," *New York Herald Tribune*, June 26, 1932.

85. "House Trades Found Easier on Long Island," *New York Herald Tribune*, October 30, 1932; "Clouds Desert Realty Horizon of Long Island," *New York Herald Tribune*, July 31, 1932.

86. Irving G. Gutterman, "Aiding the Tourist," *New York Times*, May 7, 1933.

87. "State Parkway Link Dedicated at Kew Gardens," *New York Herald Tribune*, July 16, 1933.

88. Robert J. Kennedy, "Scope of Recreation Facilities, Including Beaches, Make Long Island Clubs Outstanding Rendezvous," *New York Herald Tribune*, July 16, 1933.

89. Murray Tynan, "Piping Rock Club: Where Long Island Estate Holders Reign," *New York Herald Tribune*, August 20, 1933.

90. C. Earl Morrow, "City Streets to Forward Plan for Unrivaled Parkway System Throughout Metropolitan Area," *New York Herald Tribune*, February 4, 1934.

91. "Bill Is Passed for New Park on Long Island," *New York Herald Tribune*, August 24, 1933, 13.

92. "Moses, Apostle of Common Sense, Has Fenced with Sponsor, Won Parks Fight," *New York Herald Tribune*, September 29, 1934.

93. "House Prices Rising, Avers Wm. J. Levitt," *New York Herald Tribune*, October 28, 1934.

94. Alvin B. Wolosoff, "Dwelling Value Best Offered in Last 20 Years," *New York Herald Tribune*, January 27, 1935.

95. "Vacation House Shortage Seen on North Shore," *New York Herald Tribune*, April 21, 1935.

96. "Builders Insist Slump Is Over on Long Island," *New York Herald Tribune*, April 28, 1935.

97. "'Frost' Goes Out of Estate Sales on Long Island," *New York Herald Tribune*, February 9, 1936.

98. M.V. Casey, "Throngs Invade Long Island Villages in Biggest Housing Hunt in History," *New York Herald Tribune*, April 26, 1936.

99. "Lehman Leads 100-Car Tour of Long Island," *New York Herald Tribune*, June 3, 1936.

100. Earnest B. Bearnarth, "Aid to Travel by Triborough Bridge July 11," *New York Herald Tribune*, June 28, 1936.

101. "Long Island's New Traffic Jams," *New York Herald Tribune*, August 18, 1936.

102. "Queens Plans Roadways to Connect with Tunnel," *New York Herald Tribune*, October 1, 1936.

103. "To Montauk and Back Is Just a Nice Day's Run," *New York Herald Tribune*, November 8, 1936.

104. "2 New Parkways Go Into Use Today," *New York Times*, November 14, 1936; "New Highway Across Long Island to Link North and South Shores," *New York Times*, November 15, 1936.

105. "Long Island Pays Tribute to Moses," *New York Times*, April 4, 1937.

106. "Motor Parkway Offered as Gift by Vanderbilt to Park Systems," *New York Herald Tribune*, June 17, 1937.

107. Bert Pierce, "Through Route, Freeway Type Urged by Regional Plan Board to Utilize the Motor Parkway," *New York Herald Tribune*, July 11, 1937.

108. "North Shore Highland Area of Long Island," *New York Herald Tribune*, July 25, 1937.

109. "Area Radiates Optimism for Realty Activity," *New York Herald Tribune*, August 15, 1937.

110. "Long Island's Popular Parks," *New York Herald Tribune*, October 3, 1937.

111. "Fair Seen as Aid to Realty Values," *New York Times*, December 11, 1938.

112. Patrick J. Callan, "Callan Expects Record Upturn on Long Island," *New York Herald Tribune*, January 29, 1939.

113. "L.I. Committee Promotes Large Exhibit at Fair," *New York Herald Tribune*, September 15, 1938. See also the World's Fair Collection (LISIC).

114. M.V. Casey, "Long Island Potato Fields Sought by Building Syndicates for Home Sites," *New York Herald Tribune*, March 26, 1939.

115. Ibid.

116. "Residential Construction Shows Eastward Trend on Long Island," *New York Herald Tribune*, August 27, 1939.

117. "Builders Seek to Anticipate Cost Upswing," *New York Herald Tribune*, September 17, 1939.

Chapter 3

118. "Levitts Increase Acreage of Big House Colony," *New York Herald Tribune*, February 1, 1948.

119. "Banner Year for Builders Blocked by War with Axis," *New York Herald Tribune*, February 1, 1942.

120. Earnest B. Bearnath, "Road Progress on Long Island Will Ease Strain from Traffic," *New York Herald Tribune*, April 7, 1940.

121. "500 More Homes in the $3,000 Price Class Being Built on Long Island under FHA Plan," *New York Times*, May 9, 1940.

122. "Five Billion Dollar Preparedness Program Expected to Stimulate Realty," *New York Herald Tribune*, June 2, 1940."

123. "Booklet Issued on Attractions of Long Island," *New York Herald Tribune*, June 9, 1940.

124. Earnest B. Bearnath, "Historical Tour of Long Island Offers Attractions for Motorists," *New York Herald Tribune*, April 13, 1941.

125. "Refugees in an Old World Setting on Long Island," *New York Times*, July 10, 1940.

126. "Events of 1940 Hailed as Vital to Long Island," *New York Herald Tribune*, February 16, 1941.

127. "Private Defense Housing Active on Long Island," *New York Herald Tribune*, July 27, 1941.

128. "All Long Island Stirred by Fear of Enemy Raid," *New York Herald Tribune*, December 10, 1941.

129. Ibid.

130. "Plane Kills Man in Cemetery, Injures Six in Forced Landing," *New York Herald Tribune*, December 8, 1941.

131. "Long Island Crash Kills 5 in Bomber," *New York Times*, January 2, 1942.

132. "Survivors Describe Norness Torpedoing, Submarine Machine-Gunned Life Raft; Navy Denies Knowing of Second Sinking," *New York Herald Tribune*, January 16, 1942.

133. "New U-Boat Victim Confirmed by Navy," *New York Times*, January 17, 1942.

134. "Banner Year for Builders."

135. "Free Ways for Traffic Mark Survey of Long Island Roads," *New York Herald Tribune*, March 15, 1942.

136. "'Back-to-City' Trend Denied on Long Island," *New York Herald Tribune*, March 22, 1942.

137. "Houses Sought for Revamping on Long Island," *New York Herald Tribune*, June 28, 1942.

138. "New York Guard Bolstered by New Battalions," *New York Herald Tribune*, May 31, 1942.

139. James M. Minifie, "Full Story of Saboteur Landing; Coast Guard Thought It Invasion," *New York Herald Tribune*, July 16, 1942.

140. Jack Tait, "Famous Yachts Hunt U-Boats in High Seas Off Long Island," *New York Herald Tribune*, September 2, 1942.

141. "Crash 6,000 Feet in Air," *New York Times*, July 11, 1942.

142. "Many Big Estates Put to War Uses," *New York Times*, February 26, 1943.

143. "Kahn's Estate Leased to U.S. as Radio School," *New York Herald Tribune*, March 15, 1943.

144. "Army Moves into Harbor Hill, Mackay Estate on Long Island," *New York Herald Tribune*, July 14, 1943.

145. "O.W.I. Trains Overseas Aids on Field Estate," *New York Herald Tribune*, October 3, 1943.

146. Kerr N. Petrie, "Glen Oaks Goes to Lakeville as Army Moves In," *New York Herald Tribune*, April 1, 1943.

147. "14 Long Island Women Honored for War Activity," *New York Herald Tribune*, March 26, 1943.

148. "100 City Girls to Help Long Island Farmers," *New York Herald Tribune*, June 19, 1943.

149. "8,000 Students See Display at Mitchel Field," *New York Herald Tribune*, June 19, 1943.

150. "All State Parks on Long Island Open This Year," *New York Herald Tribune*, May 2, 1943.

151. "Active Summer Forecast for the Long Island Colonies," *New York Herald Tribune*, June 13, 1943.

152. Ibid.

153. "Long Island Resort Plans Benefits for Men in Services," *New York Herald Tribune*, June 13, 1943.

154. "Beer Shortage on Long Island Laid to Brewers," *New York Herald Tribune*, August 8, 1943.

155. "Smoked Meats Are Suggested in Shortage of Fresh Supplies," *New York Herald Tribune*, May 15, 1944.

156. "Party Fishing to Be Permitted Close to Shore," *New York Herald Tribune*, May 27, 1944.

157. "Home Builders Purchase 688 Long Island Acres," *New York Herald Tribune*, November 11, 1945.

158. "Materials Lack Curbs Building on Long Island," *New York Herald Tribune*, December 23, 1945.

159. "L.I. Parkway Project Sets Pace in Post-War Highway Building," *New York Herald Tribune*, December 2, 1945.

160. "22,067,590 Total in Parks Program," *New York Times*, February 20, 1946.

161. Jack Werkley, "U.N. Is Moving to Long Island, Gets Free Ride," *New York Herald Tribune*, August 14, 1946.

162. Bella Druckman, "The United Nations Headquarters in Long Island's Lake Success," May 19, 2021, untappedcities.com.

163. Kenneth Bilby, "Work Started at Brookhaven on First Atomic Pile for Peace," *New York Herald Tribune*, August 12, 1947.

164. John Desmond, "East to Long Island," *New York Times*, June 8, 1947.

165. Ibid.

166. Ibid. More for on Fire Island, see Jack Parlett's *Fire Island: A Century in the Life of an American Paradise* (New York: Hanover Square Books, 2022).

167. "Parkway System Will Be Extended," *New York Times*, November 29, 1947.

168. Frederick Gutheim, "Mass Building Pattern Is Set on Long Island," *New York Herald Tribune*, February 8, 1948.

169. Ibid.

170. Ibid.

171. "Large Demand for Homes in Levittown, L.I.," *New York Herald Tribune*, March 7, 1948.

172. Ibid.

173. "Financing Completed on 4,000 Remaining Levittown Houses," *New York Herald Tribune*, May 16, 1948.

174. "Six Swimming Pools Planned for Levittown," *New York Herald Tribune*, August 8, 1948.

175. "Levitts Purchase 500 Acres to Expand Home Development," *New York Herald Tribune*, August 15, 1948.

176. "Fast-Selling Dream," *Newsweek*, October 18, 1948.

177. "Land Rush," *Time*, January 31, 1949.

178. "Night Campers Line Up to Buy Levitt Homes," *New York Herald Tribune*, March 7, 1949; "Line Forms Early in Sale of Houses," *New York Times*, March 7, 1949.

179. "Land Rush."

180. "FHA Can't Prevent Negro Housing Ban," *New York Times*, March 19, 1949.

181. "Race Ban Dropped from Leases on Rented Homes in Levittown," *New York Herald Tribune*, May 29, 1949.

182. "650 Ex-GI's Sign Up for Levitt Housing," *New York Times*, August 17, 1949; Levitt maintained his blatant racist policies by not only refusing to sell house to African Americans but also by putting covenants in buyers' contracts not permitting them to resell their houses to Black people.

183. Frederick Gutheim, "Levittown Sets Up New Standards for Meeting Community Needs," *New York Herald Tribune*, June 19, 1949.

184. Frederick Graham, "Long Island Opens Frontier for Homes in Urban Revolt," *New York Times*, June 30, 1949.

185. "Builder Plans House Colony Near Levittown," *New York Herald Tribune*, July 3, 1949.

186. "Long Island Opens Frontier."

Chapter 4

187. "Levittown Rally Will Show How to Make Lawns," *New York Herald Tribune*, April 8, 1951.

188. "Veterans to Test Exchange 'Sitting,'" *New York Times*, January 2, 1950. See also the Israel Community Center of Levittown Collection (LISIC).

189. "New Store Center Features Parking and Nursery Units," *New York Times*, January 8, 1950.

190. "Levitts Purchase 30 Old Farm Sites for 1950 Program," *New York Times*, January 22, 1950.

191. "Sees Rapid Growth for Long Island," *New York Times*, January 15, 1950.

192. "Cheaper Houses Reaching Market," *New York Times*, January 19, 1950.

193. "L.I. Builders Open New Home Centers," *New York Times*, January 29, 1950.

194. "Builders Speeding Long Island Homes," *New York Times*, February 26, 1950.

195. "Group of Motion-Picture Theatres Planned in 'Intimate' Style for Levittown, L.I.," *New York Times*, March 5, 1950.

196. "Home Building Exhibit Opened by Levitt & Sons," *New York Herald Tribune*, April 23, 1950.

197. "Levitts Taking Deposits Now on '51 Houses," *New York Herald Tribune*, August 6, 1950.

198. "An Old Long Island Custom," *New York Herald Tribune*, April 15, 1951.

199. Richard H. Parke, "Nassau Epitomizes Suburban Growth," *New York Times*, August 8, 1950.

200. "Dwelling Buyer Good Prospect for Other Items," *New York Herald Tribune*, November 12, 1950.

201. "4 Say Levittown Refuses Leases After Children Play with Negroes," *New York Times*, December 5, 1950; "Levittown Fight Continues as 2 Families Ask Eviction Restraint," *New York Amsterdam News*, December 9, 1950.

202. "Bias Appeal Dismissed," *New York Times*, October 30, 1951.

203. "Sixth of Levittown Gives 3 Tons of Food in Day for Indian Orphans," *New York Times*, May 29, 1951.

204. "Boys' Teams Open Levittown Baseball," *New York Herald Tribune*, August 12, 1951.

205. "Shopping Center Playroom a Boon for Levittown Mothers and Young," *New York Times*, August 18, 1951.

206. "Levittown, All There Is," *New York Times*, November 20, 1951.

207. Richard B. Lyman, "'Levittowns' Set New Urban Pattern," *New York Herald Tribune*, November 6, 1953.

208. Ibid.

209. Ibid.

210. Harry Henderson, "The Mass-Produced Suburbs," *Harper's*, November 1953.

211. "Teacher's Right to Job in N.Y. Faces U.S. Court Test," *Norfolk New Journal and Guide*, March 29, 1952. See Mabee, *Black Education*.

212. "Negro Says Fires Won't Stop House," *New York Herald Tribune*, November 24, 1953.

213. "Fire Negro Home in Long Island," *Chicago Defender*, December 5, 1953; "Gives Up Idea to Build Home in Long Island," *Atlanta Daily World*, January 27, 1954.

214. "Did Bigots Buy Negro's L.I. Home?" *New York Amsterdam News*, January 30, 1954.

215. "Stein Starts New Homes in Freeport," *New York Herald Tribune*, March 6, 1955.

216. "New Homes Open in Long Island," *New York Amsterdam News*, March 2, 1957.

217. Oscar W. Erhard, "Builders Voice Optimism for Long Island's Future," *New York Herald Tribune*, May 13, 1955.

218. "Builders Will Modernize Glen Cove Negro Tenement," *New York Herald Tribune*, September 20, 1955.

219. "Pastor Sees New Zoning Law Leading to Long Island Slum," *New York Amsterdam News*, March 10, 1956.

220. Tom Barrett, "Negroes Integral Part of the L.I. Levittown," *New York Herald Tribune*, August 21, 1957. Oddly, an article published just one day earlier in the same newspaper reported that there were no Negroes currently in Levittown.

221. James Booker, "New York's Levittown Has No Trouble Now!" *New York Amsterdam News*, August 24, 1957. This article stated that about fifteen African American families currently lived in Levittown.

222. "Levitt Loses Housing Bias Case in N.J.," *New York Herald Tribune*, July 23, 1959.

223. Charles Loeb, "World View: Best Keep Mr. Khrushchev Away from Levittown," *Cleveland Call and Post*, August 22, 1959.

224. Herbert M. Orrell, "The Cold War and Long Island Suburbia," *Nation*, July 30, 1955.

225. "Klein Causes Jam at 'Quiet Opening,'" *New York Times*, August 16, 1955.

226. Arthur Owens, "What's Become of Levittown," *New York Herald Tribune*, September 22, 1957.

227. Orrell, "Cold War."

228. "New Deal on the Long Island," *Time*, August 1, 1955.

229. Ibid.

230. Robert A. Poteete, "Near-by Long Island Ideal for Short Auto Tour," *New York Herald Tribune*, August 14, 1955.

231. Walter H. Stern, "Builders Turning West on L.I.; Reclaim Meadows in Nassau," *New York Times*, April 14, 1957.

232. Ibid.

233. "Build Fewer, More Costly L.I. Homes," *New York Herald Tribune*, April 21, 1957.

234. "Demand Up for Custom Residences," *New York Herald Tribune*, May 19, 1957.

235. "What's Become of Levittown."

236. Ibid.

237. Ibid.

238. Ibid.

239. Ibid.

240. Ibid.

241. Cornelius DuBois, "Whither New York, Wither Bosky Dell," *New York Herald Tribune*, December 29, 1957.

242. Mauri Edwards and Florence E. Edwards, "The New Suburbanite: What's He Think of It All," *New York Herald Tribune*, March 30, 1958.

243. Ibid.

Chapter 5

244. "Ticket Trouble," *Time*, January 24, 1969.

245. Ibid.

246. Joel Goldberg, "Where Does Long Island Go from Here?" *New York Herald Tribune*, January 3, 1960.

247. Ibid.

248. "Strike on the Long Island," *Time*, July 18, 1960.

249. "The Resourceful Commuter," *Time*, August 1, 1960.

250. "Moses Calls Fair Boon to Long Island," *New York Herald Tribune*, October 16, 1960. See Samuel, *End of the Innocence*.

251. Byron Porterfield, "Across the Sound," *New York Times*, July 9, 1961.

252. Ibid.

253. Ibid.

254. Ibid.

255. Ibid.

256. Keith R. Johnson, "Builders, Realty Men Back an Anti-Bias Housing Bill," *New York Herald Tribune*, January 28, 1960.

257. "Flames Wreck Negroes' Home on Long Island," *Philadelphia Tribune*, December 10, 1960.

258. "Long Island Town Accepts New Family," *Atlanta Daily World*, July 2, 1961. For more on Great Neck, see Goldstein *Inventing Great Neck*.

259. "Soul-Searching Swank Long Island Community Drops Anti-Bias Attitudes," *Chicago Daily Defender*, July 6, 1961.

260. Ibid.

261. "CORE Offers Long Island Homes, Finds Few Takers," *Chicago Daily Defender*, November 2, 1961.

262. "Bias in Long Island Housing Protested," *Chicago Daily Defender*, December 12, 1961.

263. "Realtor Bias in Nassau—A Test Case," *New York Herald Tribune*, August 7, 1962.

264. "Integration Suits Face L.I. Towns," *New York Herald Tribune*, March 22, 1962.

265. "Slow-Footed Integration," *New York Herald Tribune*, August 1, 1962.

266. Philip S. Cook, "Suburbia Integration Push Reaches Westbury," *New York Herald Tribune*, April 3, 1962.

267. "School Roundup: NAACP Sues to Blast Long Island School Bars," *Baltimore Afro-American*, April 14, 1962.

268. "Trio Stages Racial Sit-in at Malverne Junior High," *New York Herald Tribune*, August 3, 1962.

269. "Long Island School Districts Are Named in NAACP Petitions," *Atlanta Daily World*, September 16, 1962.

270. "Negroes Will Get Chance to Change Schools on L.I.," *New York Herald Tribune*, September 22, 1962.

271. "Top Long Island Bank to Hire More Non-Whites," *Chicago Daily Defender*, January 31, 1963.

272. "Long Island Club Admits Negro; 'First,'" *Pittsburgh Courier*, October 5, 1963.

273. "CORE, NAACP Team Up in Voter Registration Drive on Long Island," *New York Amsterdam News*, March 28, 1964. See Rosen and Rosen,

But Not Next Door, and Loewen, *Sundown Towns*, for much more on the systematic exclusion of African Americans from their own communities.

274. George Barner, "Amsterdam News Task Force in Long Island: Nassau Is Most Densely Populated County, Although Suffolk Is Larger," *Amsterdam News*, January 9, 1965. Some of the county's most affluent towns had a relatively high percentage of African Americans due to the fact that they were live-in domestics.

275. Ibid.

276. Ibid.

277. "CORE Wins First Rent Strike on Long Island," *Chicago Daily Defender*, July 8, 1965.

278. George Barner, "Class Vs. Class in Long Island: The Negro Problem in Suburbs: Negroes at Odds With Each Other," *New York Amsterdam News*, December 24, 1966.

279. Joe McCarthy, "Long Island Is Becoming Long City," *New York Times Magazine*, August 30, 1964.

280. Ibid.

281. Ibid.

282. Ibid.

283. Ibid.

284. Ibid.

285. Barner, "Amsterdam News Task Force."

286. "Narcotics Expert Warns Long Island," *New York Times*, April 4, 1965.

287. "'The Island': Any Future for the Good Life?" *Newsweek*, August 8, 1966.

288. Francis X. Clines, "Long Island Searches for New Links to Mainland," *New York Times*, January 9, 1967.

289. Ibid.

290. Joe McCarthy, "Problem: The Long Island Expressway. Solution: Close Down Long Island," *New York Times Magazine*, March 19, 1967.

291. Ibid.

292. Ibid.

293. "Controversy Is Stirred by Proposals for Some Long Island Sound Bridges," *New York Times*, February 11, 1968.

294. Martin Arnold, "Why They Love That Old Long Island," *New York Times*, December 1, 1968.

295. Damon Stetson, "Long Island R.R. Commuters Show Bitterness at Hearings," *New York Times*, January 27, 1969.

296. "The Long, Long (Island) Trail," *New York Times*, July 3, 1969.

297. "Long Island Rail Road," *New York Times*, July 28, 1969.

298. "Long, Long (Island) Trail."

299. Paul L. Montgomery, "Rockefeller Considers Ousting Head of Long Island Rail Road," *New York Times*, July 26, 1969.

300. "Shake-Up on the Long Island," *New York Times*, August 1, 1969.

301. Linda Charlton, "26 Trains Canceled by the Long Island; Others Are Longer," *New York Times*, August 12, 1969; "Best Rail Road on Long Island," *New York Times*, August 14, 1969.

302. "Lifeguard Strike Still Threat for State Parks on Long Island," *New York Times*, August 25, 1969.

Chapter 6

303. Irvin Molotsky, "The New Port of Call of Drug Smugglers: Long Island," *New York Times*, July 8, 1979.

304. Philip L. Greene, "Coming of Age in the Suburbs," *Newsday*, November 21, 1970.

305. Ibid.

306. Ibid.

307. Jack Rosenthal, "The Outer City: U.S. in Suburban Turmoil," *New York Times*, May 30, 1971.

308. Richard Reeves, "Land Is Prize in Battle for Control of Suburbs," *New York Times*, August 17, 1971.

309. Roy R. Silver, "L.I. Honeymoon Cottage Just a Newlywed's Dream," *Newsday*, November 21, 1971.

310. Frank W. Corrigan, "The Money Crunch," *Newsday*, February 21, 1972.

311. Alice Murray, "On Long Island," *New York Times*, June 18, 1972.

312. Joel Mandelbaum, "Race Discrimination in Home Buying Resists Tough Laws," *New York Times*, December 3, 1972.

313. Stephen R. Davenport Jr., "The Great Ripoff of Long Island's Beaches," *New York Times*, July 30, 1972.

314. Shana Alexander, "The Last Place Left," *Newsweek*, August 7, 1972.

315. David A. Andelman, "'Condos' Get Foothold on Long Island," *Newsday*, March 18, 1973.

316. Ibid.

317. David Jacobs, "A Long View of Long Island," *Newsday*, February 17, 1974.

318. Ibid.

319. Ibid.

320. Ibid.

321. Will Graves, "We Wanted a Better Life," *Newsday*, May 5, 1974.

322. "Refugees from the Suburban Life," *Newsday*, November 2, 1975.

323. Robert Lindsey, "Less House, and More Money, For a Home," *New York Times*, December 7, 1975.

324. Kaplan, *Dream Deferred*, 23.

325. Ibid.

326. Sam Roberts, "Infamous 'Drop Dead' Was Never Said by Ford," *New York Times*, December 28, 2006.

327. Michael Drew, "…I'll Try the Island," *Newsday*, March 7, 1976.

328. Jerry Morgan, "High Cost of the American Dream," *Newsday*, September 25, 1976.

329. Ibid.

330. Ari L. Goldman, "Zoned for Contention: 2 Homes in 1 House," *New York Times*, April 25, 1976.

331. Jerry Morgan, "Your Own House—A Fading Dream," *Newsday*, March 29, 1977.

332. Andrea Aurichio, "No Place Like (Mobile) Home," *New York Times*, June 12, 1977.

333. Robert Lindsey, "Housing Boom: 2 Million Units," *New York Times*, December 4, 1977. See Samuel, *Rise and Fall of Baby Boomers*.

334. Barbara Delatiner, "Suburban Myth, Mrs. and Ms.," *New York Times*, October 9, 1977. For a historical view of women's rights on Long Island, see Naylor and Murphy, *Long Island Women*; Petrash, *Long Island*; and Naylor, *Women in Long Island's Past*.

335. Delatiner, "Suburban Myth."

336. Ibid.

337. "Quality of Life: An Exodus of the Young Threatens Life-Style," *Newsday*, March 19, 1978.

338. Ibid.

339. Ibid.

340. "Housing: High Taxes, Low Demand Hurt Values," *Newsday*, March 19, 1978.

341. Jerry Morgan, "Real Estate: Using a Bigger Slice of Wages to Buy a House," *Newsday*, October 28, 1978.

342. "Housing: High Taxes."

343. Diana Shaman, "Blueprint of the Building Crunch," *New York Times*, June 11, 1978.

344. John Knowles, "In the Hamptons," *New York Times*, June 4, 1978. See Dolgon, *End of the Hamptons*.

345. Susan Isaacs, "I'll Take Manhasset," *Newsday*, September 14, 1978.

346. Alan S. Oser, "The California Look Comes to Long Island," *New York Times*, June 8, 1979.

347. Martin Mayer, "So You Want to Buy a House," *Newsday*, August 20, 1978.

348. Morgan, "Real Estate."

349. Timothy J. McInerny, "The Ins and Outs of New Housing," *New York Times*, February 18, 1979.

350. Pat Williams and Wista Johnson, "L.I. Couple to Rebuild Fire Damaged Home," *New York Amsterdam News*, March 10, 1979.

351. Ibid.

352. Ibid.

353. Ibid.

354. "Two White Men Arrested in L.I. Cross-Burning Act," *Baltimore Afro-American*, October 6, 1979.

355. Jerry Morgan, "Living Without the Dream," *Newsday*, December 20, 1979.

356. Ibid.

Conclusion

357. W.D. Wetherell, "Have We Awaked From the 'Long Island Dream?'", *Newsday*, June 7, 1981.

358. Mitchell Pacelle, "Long Island Seeking to Retool Economy," *Wall Street Journal*, April 9, 1996.

359. National Center for Suburban Studies at Hofstra University, https://www.hofstra.edu/suburban-studies/.

BIBLIOGRAPHY

Caro, Robert A. *The Power Broker: Robert Moses and the Fall of New York*. New York: Knopf, 1974.

Day, Lynda R. *Making a Way to Freedom: A History of African Americans on Long Island*. Interlachen, NY: Empire State Books, 1997.

Dolgon, Corey. *The End of the Hamptons: Scenes from the Class Struggle in America's Paradise*. New York: New York University Press, 2005.

Dyson, Verne. *Anecdotes and Events in Long Island History*. Port Washington, NY: Ira J. Friedman, 1969.

———. *The Human Story of Long Island*. Port Washington, NY: Ira J. Friedman, 1969.

Fernhead, R.B. *Long Island: The Sunrise Home Land—Islandwide Survey of Communities, 1929*. New York: Long Island Chamber of Commerce, 1929.

Ferrer, Margaret Lundrigan and Tova Navarra. *Levittown: The First 50 Years*. Mt. Pleasant, SC: Arcadia, 1997.

Fischer, Stan. *Long Island Rail Road*. Stillwater, MN: Voyageur Press, 2007.

Gabriel, Ralph Henry. *The Evolution of Long Island, A Story of Land and Sea*. New Haven, CT: Yale University Press, 1921.

Gans, Herbert. *The Levittowners: Ways of Life and Politics in a New Suburban Community*. New York: Columbia University Press, 1967.

Goldstein, Judith S. *Inventing Great Neck: Jewish Identity and the American Dream*. New Brunswick, NJ: Rutgers University Press, 2006.

Jackson, Birdsall. *Stories of Long Island*. Rockville Centre, NY: Paumonak Press, 1934.

Kaiser, William K., Charles E. Stonier and Raymond V. Discalla. *The Development of the Aerospace Industry on Long Island*. Hempstead, NY: Hofstra University, 1968.

Kaplan, Samuel. *The Dream Deferred: People, Politics, and Planning in Suburbia*. New York: Continuum, 1976.

Kelly, Barbara M. *Expanding the American Dream: Building and Rebuilding Levittown*. Albany, NY: SUNY Press, 1993.

Kelly, Barbara M., ed. *Long Island: The Suburban Experience*. Interlaken, NY: Heart of the Lakes Publishing, 1990.

————. *Suburbia Re-Examined*. Santa Barbara, CA: Praeger, 1989.

Krieg, Joann P. *Long Island Studies: Evoking a Sense of Place*. Interlaken, NY: Heart of the Lakes Publishing, 1988.

————. *Robert Moses: Single-Minded Genius*. Interlaken, NY: Heart of the Lakes Publishing, 1989.

Kushner, David. Levittown: *Two Families, One Tycoon, and the Fight for Civil Rights in America's Legendary Suburb*. New York: Bloomsbury, 2009.

Loewen, James W. *Sundown Towns: A Hidden Dimension of Racism*. New York: New Press, 2005.

Mabee, Carleton. *Black Education in New York State*. Syracuse, NY: Syracuse University Press, 1979.

Naylor, Natalie A. *Women in Long Island's Past: A History of Eminent Ladies and Everyday Lives*. Charleston, SC: The History Press, 2012.

Naylor, Natalie A., ed. *Exploring African-American History: Long Island and Beyond*. Interlachen, NY: Heart of the Lakes Publishing, 1991.

Naylor, Natalie A., Douglas Brinkley and John Allen Gable, eds. *Theodore Roosevelt: Many-Sided American*. Interlaken, NY: Heart of the Lakes Publishing, 1992.

Naylor, Natalie A., and Maureen O. Murphy, eds. *Long Island Women: Activists and Innovators*. Interlaken, NY: Empire State Books, 1998.

Overton, Jacqueline. *Long Island's Story*. Garden City, NY: Doubleday Doran, 1929.

Panchyk, Richard. *Hidden History of Long Island*. Mt. Pleasant, SC: The History Press, 2016.

Parlett, Jack. *Fire Island: A Century in the Life of an American Paradise*. New York: Hanover Square Books, 2022.

Pennypacker, Morton. *General Washington's Spies on Long Island and in New York*. Brooklyn, NY: Long Island Historical Society, 1939.

Petrash, Antonia Petrash. *Long Island and the Woman Suffrage Movement*. Charleston, SC: The History Press, 2013).

Report of the Long Island State Park Commission. New York: The Commission, 1925.

Rosen, Harry, and David Rosen. *But Not Next Door*. New York: Obolensky, 1962.

Samuel, Lawrence R. *The American Dream: A Cultural History*. Syracuse, NY: Syracuse University Press, 2012.

———. *The End of the Innocence: The 1964–1965 New York World's Fair*. Syracuse, NY: Syracuse University Press, 2007.

———. *The Rise and Fall of Baby Boomers: The Long, Strange Trip of a Generation*. Cambridge, UK: Cambridge Scholars Publishing, 2022.

Sealock, Richard B., and Pauline A. Seely. *Long Island Bibliography*. Baltimore, MD: Richard B. Sealock, 1940.

Seyfried, Vincent F. *The Long Island Railroad*. Garden City, NY: Vincent F. Seyfried, 1968.

Shodell, Elly. *Flight of Memory: Long Island's Aeronautical Past*. Port Washington: Port Washington Library, 1995.

Silver, Marc L., and Martin Melkonian eds. *Contested Terrain: Power, Politics, and Participation in Suburbia*. Santa Barbara, CA: Praeger, 1995.

Smith, Mildred H., and Ira J. Friedman. *Early History of the Long Island R.R., 1834–1900*. Uniondale, NY: Salisbury, 1959.

Sobin, Dennis P. *Dynamics of Community Change: The Case of Long Island's Declining "Gold Coast."* Port Washington, NY: Ira J. Friedman, 1968.

Stoff, Joshua. *Aerospace Heritage of Long Island*. Interlaken, NY: Heart of the Lakes Publishing, 1989.

———. *From Airship to Spaceship: Long Island in Aviation and Spaceflight*. Interlaken, NY: Empire State Books, 1991.

Strong, John A. *Algonquian Peoples of Long Island from Earliest Times to 1700*. Interlaken, NY: Heart of the Lakes Publishing, 1997.

———. *"We Are Still Here!" The Algonquian Peoples of Long Island Today*. Interlaken, NY: Heart of the Lakes Publishing, 1998.

ABOUT THE AUTHOR

L awrence R. Samuel is a Miami- and New York City–based cultural historian and a Long Island native. He holds a PhD in American studies and an MA in English from the University of Minnesota and an MBA in marketing from the University of Georgia and was a Smithsonian Institution Fellow. His previous books include *The End of the Innocence: The 1964–1965 New York World's Fair* (2007), *New York City 1964: A Cultural History* (2014), *Tudor City: Manhattan's Historic Residential Enclave* (2019) and *Dead on Arrival in Manhattan: Stories of Unnatural Demise from the Past Century* (2021).

Visit us at
www.historypress.com